Edgar Charles Beall

**The Brain And The Bible**

The Conflict Between Mental Science And Theology

Edgar Charles Beall

**The Brain And The Bible**
*The Conflict Between Mental Science And Theology*

ISBN/EAN: 9783741134371

Manufactured in Europe, USA, Canada, Australia, Japa

Cover: Foto ©Thomas Meinert / pixelio.de

Manufactured and distributed by brebook publishing software (www.brebook.com)

Edgar Charles Beall

**The Brain And The Bible**

# THE
# BRAIN AND THE BIBLE;

OR,

## THE CONFLICT

BETWEEN

## MENTAL SCIENCE AND THEOLOGY.

EDGAR C... ...L.

WITH A ...
ROBERT G. ...SOLL.

*"Truth wears no mask; bows at ... ... seeks neither place nor applause: she only asks a hearing ... ...ruption from her teaching, though new; neither expect g... ... long believe..."*

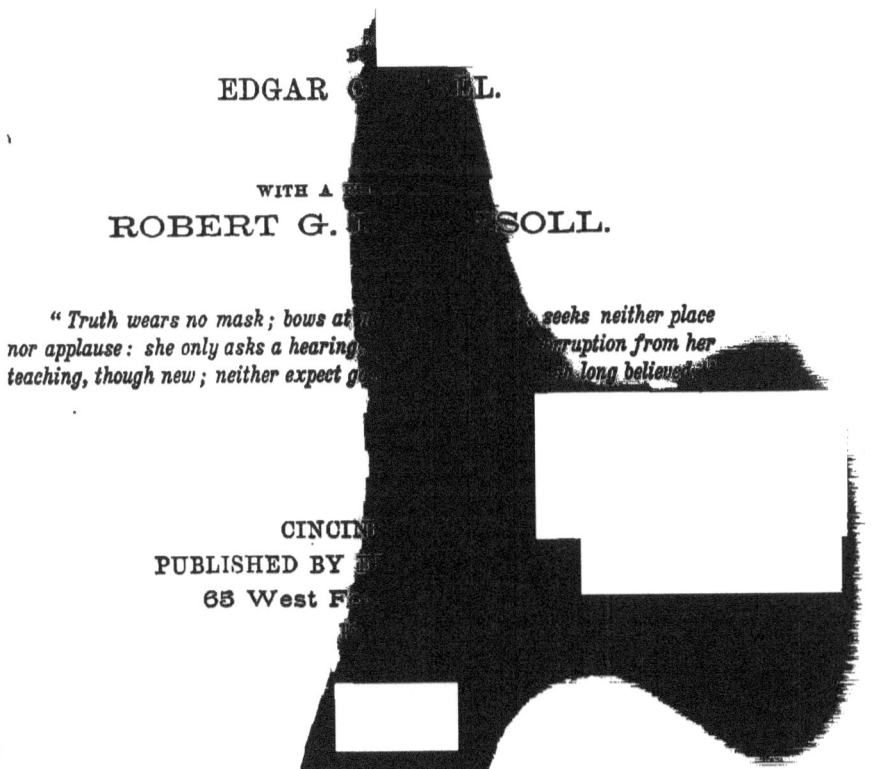

CINCI...
PUBLISHED BY ...
65 West F...

COPYRIGHTED, 1881,
BY EDGAR C. BEALL.

# CONTENTS

|  | PAGE. |
|---|---|
| DEDICATION, | v |
| PREFACE BY R. G. INGERSOLL, | vii |
| AUTHOR'S PREFACE, | xxiii |
| INTRODUCTION, | 1 |
| CHAPTER I.—THE PILOT OF THE PASSIONS, | 46 |
| " II.—THE FALL OF MAN, | 67 |
| " III.—CHANGE OF HEART, | 84 |
| " IV.—THE PLAN OF SALVATION, | 113 |
| " V.—IS NATURE SELF-EXISTENT? | 127 |
| " VI.—THE DESIGN ARGUMENT, | 140 |
| " VII.—JOSEPH COOK'S "SCIENTIFIC THEISM," | 159 |
| " VIII.—THE CORRELATION ARGUMENT, | 174 |
| " IX.—THE LOGIC OF JESUITISM, | 199 |
| " X.—POPULAR OBJECTIONS TO INFIDELITY, | 217 |
| " XI.—OUR SUBSTITUTE FOR CHRISTIANITY, | 243 |

TO ALL
FRIENDS OF HUMANITY,
WHO DO NOT FEAR TO DISCOVER IN
NATURE
THE ONLY CAUSE AND CURE
OF ALL THAT STANDS IN THE WAY OF OUR
HIGHEST GOOD,
I DEDICATE THIS VOLUME.

# PREFACE BY ROBERT G. INGERSOLL.

This book, written by a brave and honest man, is filled with brave and honest thoughts. The arguments it presents can not be answered by all the theologians in the world. The author is convinced that the universe is natural, that man is naturally produced, and that there is a necessary relation between character and brain. He sees, and clearly sees, that the theological explanation of phenomena is only a plausible absurdity, and, at best, as great a mystery as it tries to solve. I thank the man who breaks, or tries to break, the chains of custom, creed, and church, and gives, in plain, courageous words, the product of his brain.

It is almost impossible to investigate any subject without somewhere touching the religious prejudices of ourselves or others. Most people judge of the truth of a proposition by the consequences upon some preconceived opinion. Certain things they take as truths, and with this little standard in their minds, they measure all other theories. If the new facts do not agree with the standard, they are instantly thrown away, because it is much easier to dispose of the new facts than to reconstruct an entire philosophy.

A few years ago, when men began to say that character could be determined by the form, quantity, and quality of the brain, the religious world rushed to the conclusion that this fact might destroy what they were pleased to call the free moral agency of man. They admitted that all things in the physical world were links in the infinite chain of causes and effects, and that not one atom of the material universe could, by any possibility, be entirely exempt from the action of every other. They insisted that, if the motions of the spirit—the thoughts, dreams, and conclusions of the brain, were as necessarily produced as stones and stars, virtue became necessity, and morality the result of forces capable of mathematical calculation. In other words, they insisted that, while there were causes for all material phenomena, a something called the Will sat enthroned above all law, and dominated the phenomena of the intellectual world. They insisted that man was free; that he controlled his brain; that he was responsible for thought as well as action; that the intellectual world of each man was a universe in which his will was king. They were afraid that phrenology might, in some way, interfere with the scheme of salvation, or prevent the eternal torment of some erring soul.

It is insisted that man is free, and is responsible, because he knows right from wrong. But the compass does not navigate the ship; neither does it, in any way, of itself, determine the direction that is taken. When winds and waves are too powerful, the compass is of no importance. The pilot may read it correctly, and may know the direction the ship ought to take, but the compass is not a force. So men, blown by the tempests of passion, may have the intellectual conviction that they should go another way; but, of what use, of what force, is the conviction?

Thousands of persons have gathered curious statistics for the purpose of showing that man is absolutely dominated by his surroundings. By these statistics is discovered what is called "the law of average." They show that there are about so many suicides in London every year, so many letters misdirected at Paris, so many men uniting themselves in marriage with women older than themselves in Belgium, so many burglaries to one murder in France, or so many persons driven insane by religion in the United States. It is asserted that these facts conclusively show that man is acted upon; that, behind each thought, each dream, is the efficient cause, and that the doctrine of moral responsibility has been destroyed by statistics.

But, does the fact that about so many crimes are committed on the average, in a given population, or that so many any things are done, prove that there is no freedom in human action?

Suppose a population of ten thousand persons; and suppose, further, that they are free, and that they have the usual wants of mankind. Is it not reasonable to say that they would act in some way? They certainly would take measures to obtain food, clothing, and shelter. If these people differed in intellect, in surroundings, in temperament, in strength, it is reasonable to suppose that all would not be equally successful. Under such circumstances, may we not safely infer that, in a little while, if the statistics were properly taken, a law of average would appear? In other words, free people would act; and, being different in mind, body, and circumstances, would not all act exactly alike. All would not be alike acted upon. The deviations from what might be thought wise, or right, would sustain such a relation to time and numbers that they could be expressed by a law of average.

If this is true, the law of average does not establish necessity.

But, in my supposed case, the people, after all, are not free. They have wants. They are under the necessity of feeding, clothing, and sheltering themselves. To the extent of their actual wants, they are not free. Every limitation is a master. Every finite being is a prisoner, and no man has ever yet looked above or beyond the prison walls. Our highest conception of liberty is to be free from the dictation of fellow prisoners.

To the extent that we have wants, we are not free. To the extent that we do not have wants, we do not act.

If we are responsible for our thoughts, we ought not only to know how they are formed, but we ought to form them. If we are the masters of our own minds, we ought to be able to tell what we are going to think at any future time.

Evidently, the food of thought—its very warp and woof—is furnished through the medium of the senses. If we open our eyes, we can not help seeing. If we do not stop our ears, we can not help hearing. If any thing touches us, we feel it. The heart beats in spite of us. The lungs supply themselves with air without our knowledge. The blood pursues its old accustomed rounds, and all our senses act without our leave. As the heart beats, so the brain thinks. The will is not its king. As the blood flows, as the lungs expand, as the eyes see, as the ears hear, as the flesh is sensitive to touch, so the brain thinks.

I had a dream, in which I debated a question with a friend. I thought to myself: "This is a dream, and yet I can not tell what my opponent is going to say. Yet, if it is a dream, I am doing the thinking for both sides, and, therefore, ought to know in advance what my friend will urge." But, in a dream, there is some one who seems to talk to us. Our own brain tells us news, and presents an unexpected thought. Is it not possible that each brain is a field, where all the senses sow the seeds of thought? Some of these fields are mostly barren, poor, and hard, producing only worthless weeds; and some grow sturdy oaks and stately palms; and some are like the tropic world, where plants and trees and vines seem royal children of the soil and sun.

Nothing seems more certain than that the capacity of a human being depends, other things being equal, upon the amount, form, and quality of his brain. We also know that health, disposition, temperament, occupation, food, surroundings, ancestors, quality, form, and texture of the brain, determine what we call character. Man is, collectively and individually, what his surroundings have made him. Nations differ from each other as greatly as individuals in the same nation. Nations depend upon soil, climate, geographical position, and countless other facts. Shakespeare would have been impossible without the climate of England. There is a direct relation between Hamlet and the Gulf Stream. Dr. Draper has shown that the great desert of Sahara made negroes possible in Africa. If the Caribbean Sea had been a desert, negroes might have been produced in America.

Are the effects of climate upon man necessary effects? Is it possible for man to escape them? Is he responsible for what he does as a consequence of his surroundings? Is the mind dependent upon causes? Does it act without cause? Is every thought a necessity? Can man choose without reference to any quality in the thing chosen?

No one will blame Mr. Brown or Mr. Jones for not writing like Shakespeare. Should they be blamed for not acting like Christ? We say that a great painter has genius. Is it not possible that a certain genius is required to be what is called "good"? All men can not be great. All men can not be successful. Can all men be kind? Can all men be honest?

It may be that a crime appears terrible in proportion as we realize its consequences. If this is true, morality may depend largely upon the imagination. Man can not have imagination at will; that, certainly, is a natural product. And yet, a man's action may depend largely upon the want of imagination. One man may feel that he really wishes to kill another. He may make preparations to commit the deed; and yet, his imagination may present such pictures of horror and despair; he may so vividly see the widow clasping the mangled corpse; he may so plainly hear the cries and sobs of orphans, while the clods fall upon the coffin, that his hand is stayed. Another, lacking imagination, thirsting only for revenge, seeing nothing beyond the accomplishment of the deed, buries, with blind and thoughtless hate, the dagger in his victim's heart.

Morality, for the most part, is the verdict of the majority. This verdict depends upon the intelligence of the people; and the intelligence depends upon the amount, form, and quality of the average brain.

If the mind depends upon certain organs for the expression of its thought, does it have thought independently of those organs? Is there any mind without brain? Does the mind think apart from the brain, and then express its thought through the instrumentality of the brain? Theologians tell us that insanity is not a disease of the soul, but of the brain; that the soul is perfectly untouched; but that the instrument with which, and through which, it manifests itself, is impaired. The fact, however, seems to be, that the mind, the something that is the man, is unconscious of the fact that any thing is out of order in the brain. Insane people insist that they are sane.

If we should find a locomotive off the track, and the engineer using the proper appliances to put it back, we would say that the machine is out of order, but the engineer is not. But, if we found the locomotive upside down, with wheels in air, and the engineer insisting that it was on the track, and never running better, we would then conclude that something was wrong, not only with the locomotive, but with the engineer.

We are told in medical books of a girl, who, at about the age of nine years, was attacked with some cerebral disease. When she recovered, she had forgotten all she ever knew, and had to relearn the alphabet, and the names of her parents and kindred. In this abnormal state, she was not a good girl; in the normal state, she was. After having lived in the second state for several years, she went back to the first; and all she had learned in the second state was forgotten, and all she had learned in the first was remembered. I believe she changed once more, and died in the abnormal state. In which of these states was she responsible?

Were her thoughts and actions as free in one as in the other? It may be contended that, in her diseased state, the mind or soul could not correctly express itself. If this is so, it follows that, as no one is perfectly healthy, and as no one has a perfect brain, it is impossible that the soul should ever correctly express itself. Is the soul responsible for the defects of the brain? Is it not altogether more rational to say, that what we call mind depends upon the brain, and that the child—mind, inherits the defects of its parent—brain?

Are certain physical conditions necessary to the production of what we call virtuous actions? Is it possible for any thing to be produced without what we call cause, and, if the cause was sufficient, was it not necessarily produced? Do not most people mistake for freedom the right to examine their own chains? If morality depends upon conditions, should it not be the task of the great and good to discover such conditions? May it not be possible so to understand the brain that we can stop producing criminals?

It may be insisted that there is something produced by the brain besides thought—a something that takes cognizance of thoughts—a something that weighs, compares, reflects and pronounces judgment. This something can not find the origin of itself. Does it exist independently of the brain? Is it merely a looker-on? If it is a product of the brain, then its power, perception, and judgment depend upon the quantity, form, and quality of the brain.

Man, including all his attributes, must have been necessarily produced, and the product was the child of conditions.

Most reformers have infinite confidence in creeds, resolutions, and laws. They think of the common people as raw material, out of which they propose to construct institutions and governments, like mechanical contrivances, where each person will stand for a cog, rope, wheel, pulley, bolt, or fuel, and the reformers will be the managers and directors. They forget that these cogs and wheels have opinions of their own; that they fall out with other cogs, and refuse to turn with other wheels; that the pulleys and ropes have ideas peculiar to themselves, and delight in mutiny and revolution. These reformers have theories that can only be realized when other people have none.

Some time, it will be found that people can be changed only by changing their surroundings. It is alleged that, at least ninety-five per cent of the criminals transported from England to Australia and other penal colonies, became good and useful citizens in a new world. Free from former associates and associations, from the necessities of a hard, cruel, and competitive civilization, they became, for the most part, honest people. This immense fact throws more light upon social questions than all the theories of the world. All people are not able to support themselves. They lack intelligence, industry, cunning—in short, capacity. They are continually falling by the way. In the midst of plenty, they are hungry. Larceny is born of want and opportunity. In passion's storm, the will is wrecked upon the reefs and rocks of crime.

The complex, tangled web of thought and dream, of perception and memory, of imagination. and judgment, of wish, and will, and want —the woven wonder of a life—has never yet been raveled back to simple threads.

Shall we not become charitable and just, when we know that every act is but condition's fruit; that Nature, with her countless hands, scatters the seeds of tears and crimes—of every virtue and of every joy; that all the base and vile are victims of the Blind, and that the good and great have, in the lottery of life, by chance or fate, drawn heart and brain?

ROBERT G. INGERSOLL.

WASHINGTON, *Dec.* 21, 1881.

# AUTHOR'S PREFACE.

"The purpose of my writing is to make men *anthropologians* instead of *theologians;* man-lovers instead of God-lovers; students of this world instead of candidates for the next; self-reliant citizens of the earth instead of subservient and wily ministers of a celestial and terrestrial monarchy." *Feuerbach.*

THE mission of Infidelity is not to destroy any thing that is good, but simply by the light of science to discover the one sublime Temple of Truth, in search of which, groping and guessing, bruised and bleeding, humanity has wandered through all the long unhappy night of the past. Instead of wishing to undermine the principles of virtue, we seek only to make them more secure. And so far from aiming to blot out the religious nature of man, we wish only to purify and intensify it by directing it to its legitimate objects of flesh and blood.

He who can find no incentive to do right for the love of man, is incapable of sincere devotion to any noble ideal. And he who has no fear of human retribution, or hatred of wrong for its own blackness, can have but little fear of Hell. Hence, instead of an absolute, conditionless Deity, of whose existence there is no evidence, we regard Humanity as the only true object our sense of duty toward which should restrain us from evil and impel us to purity of life.

Nothing can be more sacred than the happiness of mankind, and no book sincerely written in defense of such an object should need an apology. But the Church, never willing or able to meet logic with logic, denies that Infidels aim to make the world better, and, to give color to this charge, defines Freethought as a synonym for all that is vile, and describes as its representatives only the monstrosities and dwarfs to which she herself has given birth. As to this, and all other objections, we court investigation.

All we ask is that the world may be permitted to think, and that the problem of our highest duty may be submitted to reason. Christians should not expect to discover any truth by false methods. And no greater mistake can be made than that of allowing the feelings to usurp the place of judgment. The Roman Catholic is just as sure from the voice of his "subjective cognition" that his creed is the only true one as the Protestant is that the Roman Church is the "Harlot of Babylon." But if "spiritual discernment" is superior to science, why is there so little unanimity of belief? If the "heart" is of any value as an authoritative guide, why does it present such contradictory evidence? And if the unshaken faith of millions affords any ground for an argument, why not accept Buddhism, which is believed by almost a third of the population of the globe? He who repudiates reason as the only torch, can not consistently deny that the grossest superstition may be the true religion.

However, while rejecting the solutions offered by theology, the true Infidel is far from presuming to unravel the ultimate mystery of the Absolute. "His refusal of the creative hypothesis," says Tyndall, "*is less an assertion of knowledge, than a protest against the assumption of knowledge* which must long, if not forever, lie beyond us, and the claim to which is the source of manifold confusion upon earth." Moreover, it should not be supposed that wherever Science is mute, the garrulity of Faith is necessarily true. Our inability to establish an absolute negative, by no means renders the affirmative certain; and as to the question of Theism, the burden of proof falls wholly upon the Church.

All forms of argument employed to defend the dogmas of the Bible, must, of necessity, be within a circle. Hitherto, when closely pressed, theologians have exhibited remarkable dexterity in shifting from one side of the circle to the other, and one of the chief reasons why the warfare between science and supernaturalism has continued so long, is because Infidelity has seldom attacked both sides of the circle at once. Forced by the revelations of modern physics to withdraw her lines of defense beyond the material world, the Church now seeks refuge in the supposed unfathomable mysteries of mind. It is to this field of investigation that I wish especially to call attention, and with an earnest desire to promote the highest interests not only of those who live to-day, but also of the millions yet unborn, I offer this book as a humble contribution to the sacred Cause of Humanity.

EDGAR C. BEALL.

CINCINNATI, OHIO, *December* 1, 1881.

# INTRODUCTION.

"This is truth, though at enmity with the philosophy of ages."—Gall.

"*Die einfachsten Wahrheiten sind es gerade, auf die der Mensch immer erst am spätesten kommt.*"—Feuerbach.

"*Der Stoff in seiner Gesammtheit ist die Alles gebärende und Alles wieder in sich zurücknehmende Mutter alles Seienden.*"—Büchner.

IN the infancy of humanity, the intellectual horizon was an unbroken gloom. The inexplicable every-where suggested the supernatural. The orb of day in his majestic march, the variable moon, and the serene stars, all seemed endowed with life and thought, while the voices of the genii echoed from rocks and clouds, and from wind and wave.

Although the air was filled with mystery, investigation was discouraged. To account for the miraculous by natural agencies was deemed an indignity to the gods. Science slumbered, and for many dark and weary years the great problems of life and happiness remained untouched. Anatomy and physiology were unknown. Physical disease was held to be one of the dispensations of Providence, while the realm of thought seemed directly linked with a spirit world. Temptations to commit crime were supposed to be suggested by Satan, while the disposition to be pure and good was regarded as the inspiration of Divine Grace. However, these dreams of deities and demons did not satisfy the brave few who have always dared to think, and hence the attention of the earliest philosophers became directed to a study of the human mind. For thousands of years, many of the most learned men endeavored to establish some definite system of mental science—some classification and analysis of the psychical activities which would solve the mystery of human nature. But, until near the beginning of the present century, scarcely any thing definite was ever ascertained respecting the true character of the mental organization. Theory upon theory was proposed, adopted for a while, and subsequently rejected. One after another of the great metaphysicians rose and refuted the doctrines of his predecessors, only to meet the same fate himself a few years later. But, it will be asked, why did so many seekers fail to discover the truth? Simply because of their false methods of investigation. They reasoned almost entirely *a priori*, which constantly led them into deeper mysticism. Each blindly assumed his own consciousness as the standard of human nature, and occupied himself chiefly with the contemplation of his own feelings, utterly ignoring the fact that all persons do not possess the same development of the mental powers, and that no individual could properly regard his own mind as an ideal of perfection, without first establishing the true standard with which to compare himself. Of course, every such investigator naturally evolved a philosophy corresponding simply to his own peculiar organization. For example, in the last century, the popular teleologist, Dr. Paley, who was evidently endowed with more "Veneration" than "Conscientiousness," did not admit the existence of an inherent sentiment of justice in human nature, but held that virtue consists in "the doing good to mankind, in obedience to the will of God, and *for the sake of everlasting happiness.*" This would be the natural expression of a mind in which the selfish propensities are strong, and in which reverence is more powerful than the love of right for its own sake. Looking in upon one's own feelings with such a combination of faculties, of course it would be difficult to form any other conception of moral principle. In his "*Theory of Moral Sentiments,*" Dr. Adam Smith taught that *sympathy* was probably the source of moral approbation. This idea would naturally emanate from a mind dominated by "Benevolence." Then there were writers who made the desire for praise, and various other forms of selfishness, the basis of all virtue; in teaching which they usually betrayed their own deficient sense of justice, while Mr. Stewart, Lord Kames, Dr. Brown, and many others, earnestly contended for the existence of an inherent love of justice independent of any other consideration. Equally discordant and chaotic were the opinions respecting the existence of an inherent sense of beauty; some philosophers asserting that the esthetical element in the mind was purely factitious, and acquired wholly by the post-natal experiences and education of the individual.

Scores of similar examples might be cited to show how utterly conflicting and unsatisfactory were the speculations regarding man's mental nature, when, toward the close of the last century, the functions of the brain, and the true philosophy of mind were discovered and made known to the world by Dr. Francis Joseph Gall.

Words would fail to describe the abuse and ridicule which were heaped upon this man. The Church, with her usual hostility to science, suppressed his lectures in Vienna, so that he and his companion and pupil, Dr. Spurzheim, were obliged to leave their native country in order to continue their investigations. The result of their labors, however, has been the establishment of the science known as Phrenology (a term derived from the Greek words *phren* and *logos*, mind and discourse). Dr. Gall's mode of investigation was purely *a posteriori*, or inductive. This man, a profoundly learned physician, and metaphysician, as was also Dr. Spurzheim, began his great life work when a mere schoolboy, by noticing the peculiarities of his fellow-pupils, and until stricken by death at the age of seventy-one, he continued to labor for the perfection of his discoveries. He visited hundreds of schools, prisons, hospitals, asylums, and other institutions, which afforded him excellent opportunities for observing a great many distinct types of people, of which all the individuals in each class possessed alike some one leading trait of character; and by carefully comparing the cranial developments of all such persons to whom he could gain access, he was generally able to discover, in each class, a particular configuration of brain which was equally marked in all, and which appeared to be the only peculiarity which all possessed in common. For example, in the prisons, he noticed that the heads of all the thieves were remarkably wide about an inch back of the temples, while, in other respects, they differed as much as any other class of criminals. All the murderers were remarkable for width of head just between the ears, though differing in other respects, etc., etc. In the asylums for the insane, he succeeded also very frequently in discovering a peculiar form of brain which was common to all who were deranged upon the same subject. The location of the cerebral center named Cautiousness, was discovered by Dr. Gall at an entertainment where he occupied a seat immediately behind a gentleman whose notorious irresolution and timidity had obtained for him the nickname Cacadubio. Dr. Gall was struck by the extraordinary width of this head at the point known to anatomists as the "parietal prominence," situated at the extreme upper and back part of the side head, usually about two inches from the tops of the ears. Being well acquainted with the man's predominant trait, it occurred to the Doctor that this part of the head might be the seat of a faculty of cautiousness. Accordingly, on returning home, he examined all his casts, skulls, and portraits, of which he had a large collection, and in the case of every one whose original he had known to be strongly endowed with the faculty in question, he observed a great width of head at the "parietal prominence." He next examined the heads of a number of his friends and others who were remarkable for prudence, apprehensiveness, etc., and, in every instance, he found the same configuration of brain, while in all examinations of persons who were deficient in this mental quality, he found heads narrow in the region of the "parietal prominence." Thousands of observations by later Phrenologists have demonstrated beyond a doubt the accuracy of the discovery. By these and similar inductive methods this man alone succeeded in locating twenty-seven of the forty-three centers now established; certainly one of the most remarkable labors ever accomplished by any one man. Some objectors have declared that it would be impossible for one man or one generation of men to collect sufficient evidence to establish the location of so many cerebral centers; but such critics are obviously unacquainted with the requirements of the inductive method. Dr. Gall himself made thousands of observations more than were strictly necessary to confirm his discoveries, and the centers localized by his successors have been established by millions of observations. If a coin is tossed up five hundred times in succession, or even half as many times, and it invariably falls upon a particular side, we are entirely justified in the conclusion that it is "loaded," since it would be impossible for such a number of coincidences to be accidental.

The same principle may be applied to the question of special cerebral developments. If we find that all men who possess great physico-perceptive intellectuality, with deficient reflective power, have, in every instance, foreheads very prominent immediately above the eyes, but narrow and retreating in the upper portion; while we observe that all foreheads largely developed in the upper portion and depressed in the lower, are accompanied by predominant reflective intellect, we logically infer that the perceptive faculties depend for their manifestation upon the cerebral matter beneath the superciliary ridge, and that in the upper part of the forehead are located the material substrata of the reflective powers. There is no possibility of evading the results of such reasoning. If Phrenology can not be demonstrated nothing can be demonstrated. Moreover, its leading principles are so simple that a child can easily master them, notwithstanding which, however, it is a fact that among the most learned men comparatively few understand even the rudiments of it. At first glance this seems almost unaccountable, but there are several reasons for it. First, scholars are usually very conservative, and disposed to be antagonistic to every new system of philosophy that bears an odor of empiricism, and especially if it threatens to subvert the established ideas of metaphysics or theology. Second, it is a peculiarity with the majority of philosophical minds, that they will not condescend to examine the alphabet of a candidate science, and by passing judgment upon its principles before investigating its facts, or familiarizing themselves with its technicalities, they are almost certain to arrive at conclusions exactly in accord with their preconceived opinions. Such men try to walk before they can crawl, and the result is, they accomplish but little in their investigation of a subject until they chance to become prejudiced in its favor by external influences. Third, it must be confessed that none of the phrenological treatises have ever been presented in the best manner to facilitate the study of the science. From the time when Drs. Gall and Spurzheim published their first books on the functions of the brain, to the present day, it has been customary to indicate the locations of the cerebral centers by illustrations which, to persons unacquainted with the subject, often convey the impression that the centers always exhibit visible and tangible protuberances upon the surface of the cranium; than which, however, nothing could be more erroneous. By the term cerebral "center," or "organ," as Phrenologists usually call it, is meant simply that portion of the gray or convoluted brain substance the action of which constitutes what is understood by a mental faculty. All of the centers now regarded as established, have received names which are used almost synonymously to designate either special parts of the brain, or their manifestations which we call mental faculties, and are, for convenience, written with large initials to distinguish them, as referring to individual faculties, from the manifestations which proceed from different centers acting in combination. One of the most plausible objections ever made against Phrenology, is based upon the idea that its advocates profess to have discovered forty-three distinct and independent compartments in the brain. But this is not a fair statement of their teaching. In no instance has it ever been asserted that the seats of the faculties are entirely separated, and independent of one another. On the contrary, they must be connected, and their boundaries literally interwoven like the colors in the rainbow, in order to facilitate their necessary co-operation. And yet it is quite possible that there may exist very distinct lines of demarcation which our present means of observation are too imperfect to detect. Modern anatomists show that there is really no difference in structure between a motor and a sensory nerve, except in the manner in which it terminates. A motor filament begins in a cell and ends in a kind of loop, while the sensory filament begins in one cell and ends in another. In view of such peculiarities it is not strange that the dissecting knife should fail to reveal many complex nervous functions. But while we do not profess to separate the individual fibers or cells composing each center, it is true nevertheless that the boundaries of the centers may be observed externally with sufficient exactness for all practical purposes. In cases of extreme development or unusual deficiency these limitations and consequently the shapes of the centers are very plainly discernible. As, for example, when Combativeness is very much larger than the surrounding convolutions, its form is plainly seen to be elongated, and its position perpendicular. Very deficient Continuity, when surrounded by large Inhabitiveness, Friendship, Self-Esteem, etc., causes a depression in the shape of a crescent, the points inclining downward. Other centers present still different configurations, some running horizontally and others perpendicularly. It is very difficult to understand the exact relation between brain and mind, or at least to express the idea in popular language. The German physiologist, Bock, says, "*Geist ist die Arbeit des Gehirns.*" (Mind is the labor of the brain.) Force is only a quality or property of matter, and all we can say of the mind, is, that it is the activity of the brain. For want of any more strictly accurate expression, I shall continue to use the word "center," to designate the local seat of a particular mental power, although it is to be regretted that we have not some other term which would be at once entirely philosophical and unambiguous. Now the diagrams or "mapped" heads in the phrenological treatises are intended only to show the spaces or territory which the centers occupy at the cortex or surface of the brain. These centers seem to expand from the terminus of the spinal cord upward and outward, very much as the branches and fruit upon a tree grow upward and outward from the trunk; and, *in order to estimate the development of a center, it is necessary to measure the distance from the space it occupies at the sur-*

*face of the brain or cranium, to the medulla oblongata, or terminus of the spinal cord.* A line drawn through the head from the opening of one ear to that of the other, will pass through the anterior portion of the *medulla oblongata,* thus constituting the *meatus auditorius externus,* or external opening of the ear, an entirely convenient and accurate base of measurement.

A well balanced head will, in general terms, present a development of about two-thirds forward of a line drawn upward through the opening of the ear, and one-third back of this line. After becoming familiar with this proportion it is easy to detect at a glance any variation from it. All the developments visible in the profile are measured from the opening of the ear, just as one might estimate the length of the spokes in a carriage wheel by glancing from the hub to the tire. The centers in the lateral parts of the brain, or "side head," are estimated by measuring the head through from side to side. The seats of the faculties are all double, like the eyes and ears; each faculty having a center in each hemisphere of the brain. Special prominences or elevations upon the skull are indeed sometimes produced by special developments of the brain, but this occurs only when one center is much larger than those by which it is surrounded. In like manner a depression is often caused by the great deficiency of one center when it is surrounded by others which are largely developed.

However, only a small proportion of the forty-three centers will ever be found to present such appearances upon any one head, and in all cases the development must be estimated by observing the distance from the opening of the ear to the cortex of the brain, or the surface of the skull; or by the width of the head from side to side, as the case may be. For example, to measure the center named Firmness, project a line from the opening of the ear directly upward to the top of the head, and the length of this line will indicate the development. Or, to measure Secretiveness, place the open hands upon the sides of the head about an inch above the tops of the ears, and observe the width or diameter of the head at this point. Of course considerable practice is necessary to attain skill in estimating cerebral development, as in the case of any delicate mechanical work. In this connection I may remark that the centers in the extreme lower corner of the forehead, just back of the outer angle of the eye, are perhaps the most difficult of all to estimate correctly. But it is only in exceptional cases that real obstacles are presented here, and then they are by no means formidable. The physico-perceptives, which are located beneath the superciliary ridge, are not estimated by their anterior projection alone, but also *by the appearance of the eyebrows*. Individuality, for example, which observes things simply as individual existences, is indicated not only by the fullness of the brow above the root of the nose, and by the distance from the opening of the ear, or from the most prominent part of the zygomatic arch, but also by the space between the eyebrows; while large Order causes the eyebrows to arch over the outer angle of the eyes. In general terms, the eyebrows may be said to arch over large perceptives, and to present a horizontal and flattened appearance when these centers are deficient.

*In view of these facts regarding the true methods of estimating cerebral development, all the anatomical objections to Phrenology fall to the ground.* Such as, for example, those based upon the supposed difficulties presented by the frontal sinus, the temporal muscle, variation in the thickness of the plates of the skull, etc., etc. If Phrenologists really asserted that the centers always exhibited protuberances upon the surface of the cranium, and that these excrescences must all be measured like so many warts, it would indeed be ridiculous; but they have never taught any such idea, and the popular notions regarding "bumpology" have arisen chiefly from superficial persons who criticised that which they did not understand. The same illiterate class who cry "bumpology," may generally be heard confidently discussing the "absurdities" of Darwinism. Their criticisms on Evolution may be chiefly summed up in the word "*monkey*," while the principal idea they seem to associate with the name of Dr. Gall is "*bumps.*" With reference to this latter expression, I wish to remark, in the words of George Combe, that "its use is sanctioned by neither correctness of language, nor sound philosophy."

If there is any one department of nature more important and dignified than all others, it is certainly the human brain; and whether the terms "center," and "organ," are entirely philosophical or not, there can be no need of the vulgarism referred to above. However, as the masses of the people have had comparatively little opportunity to learn much of Phrenology, it is not strange that they should often misinterpret it, or fail to appreciate it; but it is not so easy to justify the large number of eminent scientists who stubbornly oppose it. It is true we can in some degree account for their hostility, and, in view of certain reasons already indicated, they are perhaps not deserving of very severe censure; but still they ought to honor the subject of their criticisms with a careful examination. This they have obviously never done. At least it is a fact worthy of note that none of the anti-phrenological literature extant is free from gross misrepresentations, together with objections of an exceedingly trivial and irrelevant character. For example, the modern "Physico-Psychologists," "Psychic-Physiologists," or "New Phrenologists," as they are variously called, say that as the brain is like a folded glove, the functions of its midmost and lowest parts can not be known to the disciples of Gall, and that in consequence of their vivisections upon pigeons, rabbits, frogs, etc., the "phrenological map" will have to be "revised." Now this is not only unscientific, but absurd. The contributions to cerebral physiology made by these gentlemen suggest the fable of the mountain that labored and brought forth a mouse. If, for example, in the exposed brain of a dog, we discover the nerve center which enables him to wag his tail, what relation does such a demonstration bear to the exalted mental faculties of man? Suppose that by such experiments we do ascertain that a certain nervous bulb in the base of the human brain relates to the involuntary operations of digestion, respiration, circulation, etc., or to the movements of our bodies or limbs. Can this invalidate the previous discovery of such centers as Conscientiousness, Firmness, Benevolence, or Causality? By no means. As well talk of denying the existence of Jupiter because of the discovery of his moons.

There are myriads of diminutive insects whose anatomical structure has hitherto completely eluded the most skillful microscopists. If these are ever dissected and their nature thoroughly understood, will it then be necessary for us to give different names to the lion or the horse? Every science has dim recesses into which no human eye has ever peered. To this rule Phrenology has never been presented as an exception. But its advocates do profess to determine, classify, and analyze, all of the important mental faculties, in precisely the same sense that naturalists have enumerated all the important animals now extant, or in the same sense that astronomers have discovered all the important planets within the solar system.

As a proof that there yet remains but little to do in the way of discovering new cerebral centers of special importance, we submit the fact that, already, centers have been localized which, either singly or in combination, correspond to, and satisfactorily account for, all of the normal mental phenomena with which we are acquainted. As the existence and functions of these centers have been demonstrated by a rigid and extensive induction, no amount of additional discovery can ever refute them. Furthermore, clinical observation has demonstrated that they are located in the gray matter, which composes the cortex or external portion of the brain, by the circumstance that when any faculty is especially excited, diseased, or otherwise affected, the only perceptible anatomical phenomena are in the cortical substance, and not in the striated or interior structure; much in the same sense that the growth or decay of an apple is not accompanied by any perceptible structural change in the body or limbs of the tree. And as the richest fruit usually grows upon the longest branches, or at the greatest distance from the trunk, so the strength of the cerebral centers, other things being equal, is indicated more by their distance from the *medulla oblongata*, than by their lateral expansion at the surface of the brain. Hence we might as reasonably split open the limbs or trunk of a tree to look for apples, as to seek new centers of important faculties in the midmost and lowest parts of the brain. Why or how this is true, need not here be discussed. We have irrefutable proof that it is true, and that is sufficient for our present purpose. Again, if the brain may be unfolded like the fingers of a clenched hand, or glove, which, be it remembered, Drs. Gall and Spurzheim were the first to demonstrate, it is equally true that the *healthy functions* of the brain are performed only when it is *folded*, and that its most important centers may be observed without unfolding it. That this may be done is sufficiently proved by the fact that it has been done.

To show clearly and conclusively that the physiologists are, as a rule, very imperfectly acquainted with Phrenology, it is necessary only to observe the language they employ in their references to it. A single example will suffice. In Dr. Dunglison's Medical Dictionary, the edition of 1874, a well known work, and one regarded by the medical profession as second to none in authority, under the word Craniology, is the following extraordinary statement:

"According to Dr. Gall, each projection, which he calls an *organ*, is the seat of a particular intellectual or moral faculty, and all persons endowed with the same faculty, have, at the same part of the brain, a prominence, which is indicated, externally, by a bump or projection in the bony case. The *System* of Dr. Gall is made to comprise twenty-seven prominences, which answer to twenty-seven primary faculties."

Here we have the hackneyed and groundless accusation, that, "*according to Dr. Gall,*" for each mental faculty, there is in all cases exhibited a cranial "bump"; or, in other words, that each individual head displays as many bony excrescences as its owner possesses mental faculties. Truly nothing could be a greater distortion of Dr. Gall's teaching, and yet this is but a mild specimen of the misrepresentations made by many of the eminent medical, theological, and philosophical writers. I will not attempt any further explanation of the causes of this injustice. It is enough for the present to show that in this matter our opponents display either ignorance or dishonesty.

Phrenology may be defined, first, as a system of mental philosophy founded upon the physiology of the brain; and second, as the art or science of reading character by estimating cerebral power. It is well not to lose sight of this dual definition. Phrenology establishes the only correct mental philosophy by *determining the true number and nature of the primary faculties* which constitute the human mind, and in this sense it is a positive system. But as applied to reading character, it must be regarded simply as an *estimative science* precisely analogous to the practice of medicine. Until the discovery of the functions of the brain, it was impossible to ascertain the number of the inherent faculties, or to distinguish between the manifestations of distinct faculties and the manifestations produced by two or more faculties acting in concert. As, for example, if a man was observed to evince a tendency to finish every undertaking without intermission, it was impossible to determine whether this disposition arose from a faculty of executiveness, a faculty of firmness, or two such faculties in combination; or whether it was produced by a single faculty of continuity; and so with many other mental phenomena.

It may be well to explain here that the metaphysical analyses and the nomenclature laid down in many of the phrenological textbooks are not in every particular entirely correct, owing to certain difficulties which were necessarily encountered in the early history of the science, but which are now easily overcome by means of the great number of data possessed at the present time. Nearly all of the cerebral centers were first discovered by observing them in cases of extreme development, or by observing excessive or perverted mental manifestations; hence it was but natural to adopt a nomenclature, which, in some cases, was expressive of perverted rather than normal mental action. Thus Dr. Gall was led to give to the center now called Destructiveness, or Executiveness, the names "*Würgsinn,*" and "*Penchant au meurtre,*" which mean the *propensity to kill*, because he found it large in the heads of all murderers, and carnivorous animals. In like manner, the so-called "spiritual" faculties, Hope, Veneration, and Wonder, have been supposed to relate to a supernatural world, because they have been observed to be extremely active in persons strongly inclined to superstition. This inference, however, is entirely unwarranted, although it has been regarded with much more favor by modern Phrenologists than by Gall, Spurzheim, or Combe. On this point I agree substantially with Combe. The first faculty in this so-called "spiritual group," Hope, which, by many Christians, is said to inspire an intuitive belief in immortality, if regarded normally, and with reference to its dependence upon the intellect for its objects, has clearly no necessary connection with a faith in any other world than the present. The normal function of Veneration is to produce the sentiment of respect for superiors, and for every thing *pronounced by the intellect* to be great and good; also to offset the arrogance and superciliousness which would otherwise naturally spring from Self-Esteem. Thirdly, the much discussed faculty of Wonder, misnamed "Spirituality," can not be shown to have any exclusive relation to a belief in the existence of disembodied souls, or spirit communication, since it may be gratified by the contemplation of any thing novel or wonderful. Its normal function is simply to confer a love for the new and the unknown in general, and to inspire a confidence and interest in any mysterious or apparently impossible thing before the evidence of its truth has been or can be presented. It thus has a legitimate and useful sphere of activity within the domain of the natural. And as its function is clearly one of general wonder, the name of the faculty should also be a general term which could not be construed to refer exclusively to a special phase of manifestation. In discussing this subject, George Combe very correctly says, that "philosophy can not acknowledge any object or event that occurs in the present day as miraculous or supernatural: a special faculty, therefore, for belief in such objects, appears inadmissible." Again: "Philosophy does not recognize the 'supernatural,' while it admits wonder at new and extraordinary circumstances as a legitimate state of mind."

Such imperfections in the literature of Phrenology, and apparent contradictions in the teachings of its defenders, have led many to question its right to be called a true science; but this objection is entirely superficial. There are no contradictions in the science itself, and the inaccuracies of its teachers arise solely from their prejudices or imperfect knowledge. The same is true of every other department of learning.

Here it may be asked, what is the proper method by which to determine the legitimate function of a cerebral center? We answer, that the test must be made solely by our reason. If a certain sphere of activity is evidently conducive to the highest degree of *harmony in the action of the whole faculties*, the intellect and moral sentiments holding the supremacy, we may certainly regard it as legitimate. To illustrate: It is entirely reasonable to be prudent, watchful, and careful, and to try to avoid danger. We know that there are many dangers which we must escape in order to be happy, and so we perceive that the faculty of Cautiousness has a sphere of activity which is conducive to the highest degree of harmony in the affairs of life. But suppose this faculty should be too strongly developed in an individual, and should give rise to a settled hypochondria, under circumstances entirely favorable to safety, health, and happiness. In such a case it would be quite proper for the intellect to pronounce such a manifestation an abuse of the faculty. In the same manner the intellect readily perceives that gluttony, murder, theft, and lying, are abuses of Alimentiveness, Destructiveness, Acquisitiveness, and Secretiveness, because to a full-orbed and enlightened mind, these actions give great offense to the sentiments of Conscientiousness and Benevolence. Then as regards the names of the faculties, it is very evident that only those terms should be selected which will express or include all the general and legitimate functions of a faculty, without specifying any perverted manifestation or particular phase of normal action. Thus the name Wonder, adopted by Mr. Combe, is consistent with all of the legitimate functions of the faculty to which it refers, while the modern term "Spirituality" is objectionable because it implies a special phase of manifestation, which, even if it were philosophically admissible, does not include or imply the legitimate functions of the faculty within the physical world. The terms Hope, and Veneration, are, however, not open to this objection.

Phrenology thus reveals the inherent constitution of the mind, furnishing the correct ideal or model of human nature, to which all can look as an example for imitation. It bears the same relation to every thing mental, that physiology and anatomy do to the physical man. Its importance and dignity in this respect can scarcely be overestimated, although it has been objected that the true principles of government, education, ethics, etc., etc., can be ascertained without appealing to mental science, just as mathematics, chemistry, geology, etc., have been developed without any reference to the mental faculties. The fallacy of such an objection is immediately apparent when we consider that botany, astronomy, chemistry, mathematics, geology, etc., relate to objects the existence of which is entirely external to, and independent of the mind; whereas the objects of civil and criminal legislation, intellectual culture, moral philosophy, etc., etc., are the *qualities and actions of the mind itself.* These objects have, of course, no existence independently of the mind, and they can no more be systematically or correctly understood without a knowledge of the mental constitution, than surgery can be cultivated as a science in ignorance of the structure of the body.

Let us now briefly notice the subject of "Practical Phrenology," or "Anthroposcopy;" the art or science of character reading. In this sense, or from this point of view, Phrenology may be comprehended in the general term Physiognomy, although the meaning of the latter word is popularly limited to the facial organization, while the former is restricted to the cranial indications. In reading character, it is necessary to take into account not only the relative cerebral developments, but also the various modifying influences, such as health, education, the absolute size and texture of the brain, the temperament, and the "quality;" the indications of which include all facial or other physiognomical signs, and are all very perceptible to the practiced Phrenologist. Health states are comparatively easy to determine. Education, or recent activity of any part of the brain, especially if excessive, or steadily continued for a few years, or even months, produces a peculiar elevation and sharpness of the contiguous section of the cranium, a condition very easily distinguished from irregularities dependent upon other causes. Size of the brain, as a whole, or of its individual parts, is a measure of power only when the other conditions are equal. In a given temperament, and of a given texture, the larger an entire brain, or an individual part, the greater the power. All really great men have large brains, without a single exception. By great men, I mean those whose operations are on a large scale, and who deal with great subjects. Such as Shakspeare, Napoleon, Humboldt, etc. Moderate sized heads may be penetrating, subtile, and brilliant, like the diamond, but never profound; while large heads are often dull because of coarse texture or an unfavorable temperament. An individual may also manifest great intellectual power with a forehead which appears low or narrow, because of a deficiency of Agreeableness, Mirthfulness, Ideality, etc., which assist very much in giving breadth and height to the frontal lobes. Generally speaking, the most important modifying condition is Temperament. This word, etymologically considered, means simply mixture. In popular parlance, it is often used to indicate a peculiar combination of mental qualities; but as a phrenological technicality, it refers exclusively to the relative proportion of the physical elements presented in an individual, and may be taken to represent either this combination or the general state of the constitution resulting therefrom. Character is affected by temperament in several ways. First, the nutrition, activity, and strength of the brain, are dependent upon the functions of digestion, respiration, circulation, etc.; and, second, as the cerebral centers of the purely psychical or conscious activities are literally interwoven with centers relating to purely physical or involuntary functions, the great activity of any special bodily organ thus tends to excite those mental faculties which are in sympathy with its functions. Thus the condition of the digestive apparatus affects Alimentiveness, Amativeness, etc. Muscular exercise sharpens Combativeness, the physico-perceptive intellectual faculties, etc., etc.

The texture of the brain, in general terms, corresponds to the texture of the other parts of the organization, and may be conveniently determined by observing the character of the hair, skin, etc., at the same time taking into account the influence of the temperament. The especial development as well as the great activity of the cineritious or convoluted cerebral matter is indicated also by the high temperature and evident thinness of the cranial bones, peculiar adhesion of the skin to the forehead, etc., etc. Upon the texture of the gray matter depends the delicacy of the mental operations, while the absolute quantity, *caeteris paribus*, determines the power.

It is to be regretted that none of the phrenological authors give an accurate definition of "Quality." The majority of them ignore it entirely, while others confound it with the encephalic temperament, or with the manifestations of Ideality, and nearly all refer to it as a synonym for cerebral texture and consequent subtilty or power of intellect. But according to my observations, it is necessary to distinguish a condition which is not referable to any particular cerebral or temperamental combination whatsoever, and which is distinct from brilliancy or depth of intellect. This I call Quality. In popular parlance the word "blood" is often used to represent the same idea; as, for example, a family is said to be of good "blood," or good "stock." Some persons impress us by their instinctive refinement and natural aristocracy, while others, though perhaps endowed with greater acuteness or profundity of intellect, still betray a plebeian cheapness in every thing they do. High Quality is always accompanied by fine texture, but fine texture is by no means always accompanied by high Quality. The "Nervous

Temperament" of the pathological classification often illustrates very delicate texture without high Quality, while the latter is indicated by classical features, symmetrical form, etc., but especially by a peculiar stamp or expression of the face, and by a light in the eye which may be seen and felt, though not easily described.

These remarks upon mental science are of course intended only to point out the fact that the Gallian system is established, and that consequently all logical deductions from it may be accepted as irrefutable. And as it would be impossible within the limited space of this Introduction to answer all the numerous objections made by our opponents, I would ask the reader especially to remember that *the evidence upon which Phrenology rests, is of the most logical and conclusive kind known to human reason.* It challenges criticism by the most scientific methods of investigation ever devised. We do not say, look at the evidence and believe, but, look and know. However, if the reader should have any cause to doubt the accuracy of my statements, I respectfully invite him to investigate the subject for himself, which, I am sure, will more than repay him for all the necessary outlay of time and effort. I would advise a careful perusal of almost any of the standard phrenological textbooks, but particularly the works of George Combe, keeping in mind the hints I have given in the preceding pages with reference to the proper methods of measuring the cerebral developments, as well as regards the scientific analysis of the faculties of Hope, Veneration, and Wonder. But if this should prove insufficient to convince the skeptical student, let him observe the heads of his friends and others as he has opportunity, and if he conducts his investigations according to the rules to which I have referred, he will certainly discover that the "Doctrine of Gall" is supported by an array of facts which nothing can set aside. And who can contentedly remain unacquainted with a subject which is confessedly second to none in dignity and importance? It can not be denied that with the recognition of Phrenology, deductions fatal to all the popular systems of mental and moral philosophy are inevitable. That this is not an idea held by Infidels alone, the reader may easily assure himself by referring to the writings of almost any of the orthodox metaphysicians from Sir William Hamilton to Dr. McCosh. As a characteristic acknowledgment regarding the Gallian philosophy, take the following from an anti-phrenological work by the late Rev. Dr. Rice, of Cincinnati: "If its fundamental principles are true, every other system of mental and moral science must be not modified and improved, but absolutely abandoned as utterly false. Locke, and Reid, and Stewart, and Brown, and all others must be forever laid upon the shelf."

To this and similar admissions by theological opponents, however, it may be objected that many of the clergy are followers of Gall. Very true; but it may be regarded as equally certain that no theologian can be a scientific Phrenologist unless he is heterodox in his theology, and that no Phrenologist can be orthodox in theology unless he is very unscientific as a Phrenologist.

But while I earnestly defend the true Phrenology, I by no means indorse the many itinerant self-styled Professors, who, in all parts of the country, are preying upon the curiosity and credulity of the public, and who, although with good intentions perhaps, succeed only in bringing this noble science into ill-repute. Many of these persons have never received any instruction from a master of the subject, and are even unacquainted with the most important phrenological literature. However, this is largely the fault of the public. There would be a greater number of good Phrenologists if the people would patronize them. The quality as well as the quantity of the demand is likely to regulate the character of the supply in every thing.

Scarcely any thing is more susceptible of quackery than "Practical Phrenology," and no mere beginner should ever attempt to read character professionally, any more than a tyro in surgery should attempt to extract a cancer.

But still it is very wrong to judge a science merely by its representatives. Character and reputation are often very widely different. Phrenology is not the property of Phrenologists. It belongs to the whole human race, and appeals to every individual. If the people want better Professors of mental science, let them make the demand, and it will be met. Or if the people want better phrenological treatises, let them free their minds from the slavish dogmas of supernaturalism, and the phrenological textbooks will be correspondingly improved also. *It is the superstition in the world to-day which keeps scientific Phrenology in obscurity.* When the clouds break away the sun will appear.

Hoping that the reader may be prepared to accept the ideas contained in the subsequent chapters at their just value, whatever it may be, I shall proceed with a few arguments to show that the Brain is the only true Bible; that Nature embraces all there is of which we have any logical evidence, and that neglect of Nature paves the broad road to the only Hell, while obedience to natural law makes a flowery path to the only Heaven.

## CHAPTER I.

### THE PILOT OF THE PASSIONS.

IN surveying the mental constitution we are struck by the fact that the different faculties are not all of the same rank or importance, and that some of them are adapted to be leaders and directors of the others.

Abundant experience shows that mankind are happiest when acting under the supreme control of the moral sentiments and enlightened intellect. That is, allowing to each of the lower propensities a sphere of activity which shall be pronounced by the intellect to be legitimate, and which can give no offense to the moral sentiments. The propensities are entirely blind, simply desiring gratification, without the least power to determine their proper objects. Thus, for example, Alimentiveness simply desires food; but the assistance of the intellect is necessary to decide as to what is wholesome. Acquisitiveness, if indulged without any reference to the decisions of the intellect, would be as much gratified by the accumulation of stolen property, as by the proceeds of a legitimate business. Benevolence is quite as blind as Alimentiveness. It simply prompts to deeds of kindness, and, unless controlled by intellect and Conscientiousness, would be delighted to steal from the rich in order to help the poor. In fact this manifestation is by no means infrequent. Conscientiousness, although itself such a powerful element for good, and so necessary for the control of the other faculties, is also entirely dependent upon the intellect for guidance. Indeed nothing can be more obvious than that in every age and clime, people have been educated to do wrong in the firm belief that they were fulfilling their highest duty.

Now, the faculty of Veneration, like the appetite for food, can not of itself suggest an object which shall deserve its homage. If it can be superior to reason, why have the religious nations of the world always worshiped deities which corresponded exactly in character to the peculiar intellectual status of their votaries? That Veneration must be directed through the intellect to its objects, is too self-evident to require any extended illustration.

The faculty of Wonder, miscalled "Spirituality," as I have stated in the Introduction, has been regarded by many as properly the faculty of faith in the supernatural, and particularly in the Christian Bible. But if it has the power to select its objects, why is it stimulated by cognitions and beliefs which vary as interminably as the intellectual training and biases of its possessors? As, for instance, among Mohammedans we find it excited and gratified by the Koran, although unaffected by the traditions of Buddhism. Among the Jews we find it marveling at the fables of the Pentateuch, although indifferent to the alleged miracles of Christ; while among Roman Catholics and Protestant Christians its phases of manifestation present still different peculiarities, which, in some respects, are diametrically opposed to each other and to those of all other creeds. The cold intellectual act of belief, combined with the influence of this faculty, constitutes "faith;" but alone, Wonder produces simply a pleasurable emotion when any remarkable circumstance is communicated to the mind. As its gratification depends solely upon the novel or extravagant character of certain objects contemplated by the intellect, it may be said to stimulate or produce belief in those objects, from the fact that *it repels every act of the intellect which would divest them of their marvelous qualities.* Thus, when an individual has been taught to believe the reputed Christian miracles, a large development of Wonder, by filling the mind with agreeable sensations awakened in consequence of that belief, in its turn, biases the judgment in favor of the reality and legitimacy of the miracles. It is thus clearly impossible that this sentiment can possess any superiority over the intellect as a guide to truth, when from its very nature it must antagonize all attempts to destroy the phantoms upon which it feeds. Independently of intellectual cognition, it is no more able to solve the problems of the Whence and Whither, or to teach us the duties of life, than the avarice of a miser, or the egotism of a tyrant.

As regards the remaining one of the so-called "spiritual faculties," Hope, I have already remarked that it is thought by many to be the basis of the almost universal belief in the immortality of the soul, and therefore an indirect proof that there is a future life. There are, however, no facts to support the assumption that Hope, unaided by external evidence presented to the intellect, would instinctively suggest a belief in a spirit world. The true office of this faculty, regarded by itself, is simply to produce a feeling of confidence in the future attainment of whatever the other faculties may desire, without any reference to possibility, probability, or reasonableness. Hence, to assert that these three faculties possess within themselves an intelligence which can determine the reality of certain objects, the existence of which is declared by the intellect to be impossible or incredible, because in direct conflict with the first principles of scientific and philosophical investigation, is as irrational as to say that the paintings of Rembrandt or Titian can delight the blind, or that the symphonies of Beethoven can thrill the deaf.

That these faculties have for many ages been exercised to a great extent in connection with a belief in the supernatural, may be easily explained. The function of Wonder, as before stated, is to inspire in the mind a sympathy with any thing new, remarkable, or apparently inexplicable, under circumstances where demonstration is for the time being impracticable or difficult. This love for the unusual, the extravagant, and the romantic, relieves the mind of that staid, matter-of-fact tendency, which may often be observed among individuals of all ranks, and manifestly serves a very useful purpose in offsetting what would otherwise be a too skeptical and disagreeably incredulous action of the intellect. Without a certain degree of this element, the mind is almost as prone to sneer at new and extraordinary scientific truths, as to reject the supernatural. The faculty of Veneration naturally reveres the ancient, the powerful, and the good, thus producing the disposition to recognize and submit willingly to authority. Its influence, when predominant, is well illustrated in the sycophantic character of the negro; while the American Indians, who have a great deal of Combativeness, Destructiveness, and Self-Esteem, bow to no one but the "Great Spirit." Hope, in its normal action, looks to the future, and directs the mind to a contemplation of possible enjoyments beyond the present.

By comparing these facts of normal mental function with the history of religious creeds, it is very evident that the whole structure of supernaturalism, with all its beauties and terrors, has been developed from an abuse of the mental faculties rather than by an obedience to the true Bible of Nature.

In the dawn of intellectual evolution, nothing was known respecting the constitution of the mind, and little more concerning the facts of the external world. Consequently, the mental faculties operated merely as blind instincts, simply desiring gratification, without the slightest regard to any laws of mental action. Inexplicable phenomena were observed on every hand. All operations of nature not visibly connected with their causes, appeared to depend upon some capricious being superior to nature. Thus was first suggested the idea of a God. A desire to secure the approval of the gods, and to avoid giving them offense, was the foundation of all religious worship; and this explains why systems of theology are almost as old and as universal as ignorance itself. As the gods were conceived to be the highest powers in the universe, of course they became the chief objects for the exercise of the faculty of Veneration. All phenomena, or accounts of phenomena, supposed to proceed from the gods, naturally afforded the most accessible and abundant material for the gratification of the faculty of Wonder. The connection of the faculty of Hope with the idea of immortality, originated in the same manner. A purely intellectual process determined the belief in the permanency of the supposed psychical entity, and the faculty of Hope seized upon this conception as the highest object for its gratification, and finally came to be regarded as the source of the idea.

We are thus led to the conclusion that the intellect is the only possible judge of what constitutes legitimate food for the various mental powers,—in short, that reason bears the same relation to the propensities and sentiments that the engineer of a locomotive does to the steam in the boiler. And if this is true, we must admit that *no object is worthy of our respect or our belief, if it is declared by our enlightened intellect to be false.*

It is often objected that reason is not infallible. Suppose it is not. Does that in any degree change the fact that it is the only proper guide for the whole faculties? Would any one think of denying that it is the duty of the engineer to regulate the locomotive, simply because his judgment is not always correct? Certainly not. We always consciously or unconsciously evolve our beliefs from evidence presented to the intellect, be they what they may, simply because it is only the intellect which does believe. And yet, while belief is restricted to the understanding, of course the instinctive activity of the other faculties often biases its judgments. Thus the blind sentiments of Wonder, Veneration, and Hope, may incite the intellect to seek out objects for their gratification, although within themselves they are utterly unable to form any ideas, and are helplessly dependent upon the intellect for all the objects they secure. But, to obtain the highest results, all tests of truth should be made by intellects which are trained to logical methods, and which are *duly enlightened regarding the legitimate spheres of all the propensities and sentiments.*

Some clergymen of to-day who imagine that Phrenology may be reconciled with Orthodoxy, lay great stress upon the idea that fragmentary heads always evolve fragmentary philosophies, and hence that men of ever so great intellect who are deficient in Veneration, Wonder, and Hope, are incapable of ascertaining the higher needs of the soul, or of properly criticising the Bible. But it might quite as reasonably be objected that a skillful pilot is no longer capable of determining the safest course for a ship when in a storm, simply because at such a time all her sails are furled. However, while we hold that these angular philosophers are fully able to point out the perilous rocks and strands in the ocean of life, we freely admit that before they can be thoroughly qualified to suggest the necessary motors for the ship of humanity, they must become acquainted with the legitimate functions and needs of the whole mental faculties. But it is a very great error to suppose that all Infidels are only angular iconoclasts. It is simply a question as to the true religion; that is, as regards the proper ideals to which mankind should be bound; and as to whether we should be guided to our ideals by reason, or by emotion.

Now we are taught by supernaturalists who profess to be authority in matters pertaining to the highest culture, that "all things are possible with God," and that it is our duty to believe in the divinity of the Bible whether we can reconcile its doctrines with reason or not. But if the objects of our belief are not to be subjected to logical criticism, why should Christians not accept Mohammedanism as the true religion? Indeed, why is not the Koran the true Bible? The Christian answers, "because it teaches absurdities, impossibilities, etc.; such as that the earth is a level plane; that the sky is supported by mountains, etc." Now I ask, if "spiritual discernment" is superior to reason, what right have we to reject the Koran on the ground that it is unreasonable? May it not have been a part of God's "infinite and unfathomable plan," to introduce those inconsistencies into the Koran just to "try our faith"? How shall we decide, if all things (absurdities included,) are possible with God? But if we test the Koran by the standard of reason, why should we not subject every other Bible to the same test? The Christian of course scorns Mohammedanism, Buddhism, etc., etc., as systems destitute of any logical support, and hence unworthy of acceptance; but is not this an appeal to reason? Christians often admit that the truth of their religion can not be demonstrated by logic, and yet they say they choose it in preference to Buddhism, or other heathen superstitions, because it is *better* than the latter. But how do they determine that it is "*better*," if not by an operation of the intellect? Are they not, therefore, very inconsistent in denying to the Infidel the right to test their Bible by the standard of enlightened intellect, when they do so themselves according to their ability? Clergymen may often be heard preaching this idea: "If the difficulties in the Bible will not yield to our reason, *then our reason must be defective.*" But how can a man be justified in the conclusion that, in such a case, his reason is at fault, until he has first demonstrated that the Bible is true? And how is it possible ever to demonstrate the divinity of the Bible, so long as it can be shown to contain doctrines which are utterly opposed to reason? Why not say, "if the Koran contains apparently illogical statements, then my ideas of logic must be defective"?

To deny that a creed must be subjected to reason, is equivalent to saying that there is no means by which to distinguish truth from error, since it is only through reason that we know any thing. And to admit that a book contains statements which are irreconcilable with reason, must be equal to an admission that the book is not divine.

To show that Christians themselves, as long as was possible, held that in order to be authoritative, the Bible must be true in all its details, it is necessary only to point to their tireless efforts to explain the inconsistencies in which it abounds. And that no theologians would ever have modified the doctrine of plenary inspiration if the demonstrations of science had not compelled them to do so, is too self-evident to require any illustration.

And now I would ask, is not the Christian Bible unreasonable, and unworthy of acceptance as anything more than a human literature? To prove that it is not an infallible book, and that its very foundation is at utter variance with truth, we have only to compare its declarations with the certain revelations of nature. Subjected to the crucible of logic, nothing can be clearer than that the Bible has been produced within the realm of the natural; that it is simply human; that it abounds in error, and that it only illustrates the mental development of the times in which it was written.

It is often asserted that we are daily obliged to admit many things in nature as true which are beyond and above our comprehension; as, for example, the growth of vegetation; the phenomena of heat, light, electricity, and human life itself. And as these and a thousand similar inexplicable truths are believed without question, we are told that we should not reject the mysteries of the Bible. To this, we reply that the mysteries of nature, although not explainable by human intelligence, are still in *harmony* with reason and experience, while the dogmas of the Bible are flatly *contradicted* by reason. As there is no analogy between the two cases, this objection, together with all others of its kind, falls to the ground. Again, it is urged by many, that because the theory of Evolution is not yet positively demonstrated, and because we can not *trace* the first appearance of life upon the earth —in a word, because Science has been unable to disintegrate the Absolute, she should humbly bow at the shrine of Christian Faith, and acknowledge herself a learner at the feet of Superstition. But how absurd is this insinuation that because Science has failed to do *every thing*, she has therefore done *nothing!* Is it necessary that a gallon should be a hogshead in order to be more than a gill? Why, then, should the evidences supporting the theory of Evolution need to be presented in an endless chain, without a missing link, simply in order to outweigh the "airy nothings" of Bible creeds? As to the mysteries of the objective world, Infidels have always been the first to admit that all our knowledge is simply relative, and that the nature of things "*an und für sich,*" must forever remain inscrutable to our finite minds. All we affirm, and all we insist upon, is, that fact is weightier than fancy; that knowledge is superior to faith and fear; that only reason can safely guide us in our investigations, and that the achievements of Science, although imperfect, are infinitely more than sufficient to render incredible the dogmas of the Church.

But theologians are not content with simply ridiculing our "Gospel of Dirt," as it has been called. And they not only assume that our inability to bridge the chasms between the known and the unknowable should be taken as proof that theology is true, but that before we reject the theological affirmative, it is our duty to prove our negative. That is to say, before we reject the Bible, it logically devolves upon us to demonstrate absolutely that there is *not* a supernatural order. Could any thing be farther from all principles of correct reasoning? Suppose an innocent man is arrested on a charge of theft. Must he be punished simply because he is unable to prove an *alibi*? No; the court must hold him innocent until he is proven guilty, and unless the evidence of his guilt is presented, he is entitled to an honorable dismissal. The same is true of Infidelity. For eighteen centuries Freethinkers have been arraigned before the bar of Christian Ecclesiasticism, on the charge of criminal unbelief, and it devolves upon the Church to produce the evidence of our guilt. This she never has done, and never can do. Therefore, while we do not say *absolutely* that our honest heresy is no crime against some infinite and unknowable Being, *in the absence of any logical evidence* of such a preposterous thing, we simply do not, can not, and should not believe it.

Objections are also made against criticism of the Bible, on the ground that its chronology, geology, astronomy, etc., etc., are not inspired, and were not intended to be scientifically correct. But who has the authority to say that one part is true and another false? If the story of Eden is a "poem," a "picture," or an "allegory," as we are often told, why may not the command to believe in Christ be also an "allegory?" Why may not the doctrine of Eternal Retribution be a "picture?" Or why may not the whole Plan of Salvation be a "poem?" If Genesis is not a "geological book," and was not intended to give a "scientific" account of the creation of the earth, how shall we know that it was intended to give a "scientific" or literal account of the fall of man? The Christian may answer that the Bible is simply a moral guide, and that it is infallible only in its exposition of moral science. But, unfortunately for this position, there are as grave errors in the moral science of the Bible as there are in its astronomy, geology, ethnology, etc. There is, therefore, no way here for the Christian to escape an embarrassing dilemma. If the Bible is to be taken as a message from God, we must accept it as entirely divine. There can be no middle ground in the matter. If it is inspired, its authority must rest upon its infallibility. If we can show it to be false in certain particulars; if we can point out errors in certain parts, it then becomes subject to the decisions of our intelligence as to the truth of all its parts, and necessarily loses all its authority. However, our present inquiry has to do solely with the truth of the fundamental doctrines of the Bible, and if we can show that these are opposed to reason, they must still be unworthy of our belief whether they are inspired or not.

## CHAPTER II.

### THE FALL OF MAN.

IF Adam ever existed in reality, it will hardly be denied that his cerebral organization must have been either complete or incomplete; perfect or imperfect. If complete, and perfect, his brain would have presented a harmonious configuration, and a development chiefly in the upper and frontal regions. Furthermore, if a perfect brain ever existed, it must have produced a perfect mind.

A perfect mental organization would be, of course, one in which all the various faculties would act harmoniously, the intellect and moral sentiments holding the supremacy.

Now, if Adam was created perfect, his lower propensities must all have been entirely under the direction and control of his intellect and his moral sentiments, and, consequently, no thought, no desire, no action, could have found sympathy in his mind unless approved by his moral sentiments and intellect.

All eminent orthodox writers agree that "sin" is sympathy with what is known to be wrong; a yielding or consent of the mind to sympathize with, or to do, something which the intellect decides is not right. No intelligent definition of sin can be given which does not agree with the one just stated. To say that a man commits a sin without being aware of it, is absurd. He may, indeed, unconsciously do wrong, that is, do an act which is in some way harmful; but as long as his intentions are right and his thoughts pure, he can not be said to sin.

If, by the words "perfect government," we mean any thing, we certainly mean at least a government which would not consent to a violation of its established laws. And if the words "perfect moral nature" have any significance, they certainly imply a combination of mental powers in which it would be impossible for any of the lower faculties to act without the approval of the higher. For illustration, we know that there are thousands of persons who could never obtain the consent of their Conscientiousness and Benevolence to commit a willful murder. Why not? For the same reason that an ounce can never outweigh a pound.

A perfect mental organization then, from a moral point of view, would be one in which Conscientiousness and the other moral faculties would exercise the same restraining power with reference to all the lower propensities, that they do in the case of the best people now in the world, with reference to the crimes of murder and theft. If a man can not possibly obtain the consent of his mind to commit a theft, he may be said to have a perfect moral nature so far as that particular crime is concerned. In fact, nothing is more frequently observed than a disposition on the part of individuals to indulge readily in certain peculiar vices, while they would scorn to do other reprehensible things to which some of their neighbors would probably yield with scarcely any power of resistance. Thus, one man will indulge in excessive gluttony and drunkenness, and yet will abhor stealing. Another will steal, and yet will rigidly obey every physical law. The former would be a perfect character so far as theft is concerned, and the latter would be perfect so far as the abuse of appetite is concerned; while an entirely perfect mental nature would preclude the possibility of any vice or crime whatsoever.

If Adam was created perfect he could not have sinned, because none but an imperfect nature can sympathize with wrong. If he was morally perfect at all, his perfection must have consisted in the supremacy of his moral faculties, and in a necessary incapacity to yield the reins of government to the lower propensities. And if his moral faculties had been supreme, his highest pleasure would have been in acting according to their dictates. It is, therefore, unreasonable to believe that such a man was ever created perfect, and that, notwithstanding his perfect moral powers, he allowed the lower nature to overcome the higher.

The idea of a perfect moral nature necessarily implies a complete moral restraining power; and where this moral restraint is perfect, no amount of temptation would be capable of overruling it. Such a mind would be as incapable of vice as Nero was incapable of virtue. Imagine Nero being irresistibly tempted to a life of purity! Could any thing be more absurd? And yet it is surely no more inconsistent than to imagine a perfect man and woman being induced to steal.

If it is objected that in a perfect mental organization, the lower faculties would be subject to the same temptations as in any other combination, I answer, that from the very nature of the case, the greater the appeal to do wrong, the greater would be the offense to the moral sentiments; and as in a perfect supremacy of the moral forces, all sinful appeals to the lower propensities would elicit a corresponding resistance from the moral sentiments, of course the intensity of this resistance would keep pace with the force of the appeals to the lower faculties, thus entirely preventing the lower propensities from ever obtaining the consent of the moral faculties to indulge a criminal desire. Take, for example, a highly cultivated and refined lady, with large Benevolence, Conscientiousness, etc., and with small Destructiveness and Acquisitiveness. Think of such a person being tempted to commit a murder for the purpose of robbery. That is, imagine her debating the question in her mind; her small Destructiveness and Acquisitiveness urging her to commit the deed, and her moral faculties protesting against it. With such a combination of faculties could there be any conflict in the mind, any debate, any temptation (i. e., tension)? It would surely be an argument of only one side; a simple decision of the moral faculties. The bare mention of so terrible a crime would shock such a nature. Now, if the reader will picture to himself a mind in which the moral faculties exert a similar restraining power over all the inferior propensities, he will have the idea of a perfect mental government.

If Adam possessed such a perfect mental equipment, he would not and could not have sinned, because *perfection implies complete moral restraint.* On the other hand, if he was created imperfect, in yielding to sin, he would have undergone no constitutional change. That is to say, if he sinned in deed, he was a sinner in thought before he committed any outward act, and must have been originally endowed with a sinful nature. Or, in still other words, he must have been depraved before he fell, or he would not have fallen, and being already sinful, of course did not fall when he sinned.

The Bible teaches that Adam fell. If he was created perfect, the idea of the Fall is absurd. If he was created imperfect, he then, in sinning, simply acted out the nature with which he was endowed, and manifested a will which was necessarily evolved from his inherent organization and his environments. In the latter case, God would have been directly responsible for Adam's transgression. This can be shown more clearly, however, after a definition of the will.

The mental faculties may be compared to the members of a jury or any legislative body. When a juror suggests a certain verdict, or a legislator proposes a bill, its adoption or rejection depends upon the relative strength of its supporters and opponents. The operations of every individual mind are precisely analogous. When certain faculties approve, and others oppose, a sort of debate or conflict ensues, and the result is the will. This result, or decision, stands in the same relation to the faculties that the verdict of a jury does to the jurymen, and is not by any means itself a faculty of the mind, as is popularly supposed.

## THE FALL OF MAN.

Some quibblers try to make it appear that the will is a faculty of the mind by using the word faculty in the sense of indefinite ability or power. And because the mind has the capacity or power to evolve certain wills, or resolves, they say that it has the *faculty* to do so, and hence that the will itself is a faculty. This is, however, a very flimsy piece of sophistry. In the phrenological sense, the word faculty refers only to a mental manifestation which proceeds from a single cerebral center, or individualized part of the brain, as distinguished from combined activities. Thus, Acquisitiveness is a distinct faculty, while selfishness is not.

The will is always determined by the strongest faculties; either those which are permanently strongest, or those which are for the time being strongest. For example, a merchant wills to go to a distant city to buy goods. He is prompted to do so by predominant Acquisitiveness; the other faculties giving their consent to this gratification of the leading propensity.

But just as he is about to start upon his journey, he learns that a malignant fever has suddenly appeared in the city, whereupon he is so alarmed at the prospect of danger, that he immediately resolves, or wills, to remain at home. Now, in this case, the merchant has a great deal of Cautiousness, as well as Acquisitiveness, and the former being suddenly excited, overrules Acquisitiveness and reverses the will. Surely nothing could be simpler than this, and yet, for centuries, philosophers have been trying to prove that the will is a faculty of the mind, and entirely free.

Nothing is more erroneous than the supposition that one can will to do any thing independently of his faculties. However, the objection is often made that a man may have, for example, a strong proclivity to steal, which, though his master passion, he overcomes by an "effort of the will." But let us examine this so-called "effort of the will." We find, perhaps, that the man has very large Approbativeness, which makes him so keenly sensitive to the opinion of his friends, that the fear of disgrace and loss of social position produces a feeling much stronger than the desire to steal. Or, he may be restrained by large Conscientiousness. The result is, he does not and can not obtain the consent of his whole mind to commit the crime of theft. Besides, he may be endowed with great Firmness also, which bestows the quality of persistence and steadfastness in a position once taken. This faculty may be defined as the propensity to resist all influences tending to produce changes of purpose, and is the basis or source of the mental quality popularly known as "will power." Among the innumerable misconceptions in regard to mental science, perhaps none is more common than to confound the idea of will with that of "will power," or Firmness. A person may be almost totally deficient in "will power," and yet have as may wills as one endowed with the highest degree of Firmness. If there should be any difference, the individual with small Firmness, on account of his vacillating character, would be likely to evolve a greater number of wills than the other.

The idea of a freedom possessed by every individual to evolve *a* will, is, by the advocates of "free-agency," strangely confounded with the idea of a freedom to evolve *any* will, than which nothing could be more illogical. Of course, every one is free to will to do whatever he is free to resolve to do, but it is certainly impossible for him to will what he can not choose; that is to say, to wish what he can not desire. Now the theologians say that Adam was created a "free agent," and that he was perfectly free to sin or not to do so, but that he chose to sin. And their only explanation of his motive in choosing to sin, is, substantially, simply "*because he willed to do so.*" If we ask why he "*willed*" to sin, they answer "*because he chose to do so.*" No one who will allow himself to analyze this singular doctrine can fail to see that it is utterly opposed to reason.

The Church says that any man is free to live a life of piety, "if he only will." Very true, "if he only will;" but suppose he can not will. Suppose his animal nature is always stronger than his moral faculties. "Ah!" says the supernaturalist, "but he can *will* if he only *resolves* to do so." This is equivalent to saying that a man would be perfectly free to fly *if he only had wings.*

Freedom can be defined only as a condition which is *unaccompanied by restraint*. The less restraint, the more freedom; and *vice versa*. It matters not in what form the restraint may be exercised, whether by bolts or chains, by the " silken cords of love," or by the lash of Conscientiousness. Perfect freedom can exist only where there is an absence of all restriction, and if, as the Church teaches, Adam was perfectly free to sin, *he could not have possessed any moral faculties whatever;* which, supposing him to have been a perfect man, is, of course, the climax of absurdity.

Modern Calvinists hold that there is a radical distinction between necessity and certainty. And while they do not teach that God decrees human volitions in such a sense as to make them *necessary*, they assert that he endows men with such tendencies, and surrounds them with such environments that they will be *certain* to act just as they do. They say also that the elect *can* fall away after regeneration, even totally and finally, but never *will*. Now can any theologian explain how it is possible to provide for the certain accomplishment of a result, without interposing conditions the effects of which will be inevitable? And if those conditions inevitably produce the desired result, is not the result a *necessary* effect of those conditions? What constitutes certainty in a result, if it is not the necessary relation between cause and effect? How can God know that the elect never will fall away, unless he is aware of certain conditions which would render it impossible for them to do so? And since the predominant faculties of the human mind necessarily determine its volitions, how can those volitions be said to be free?

One of the chief reasons, perhaps, why people cling to the doctrine of "free-will," is because every one is conscious of a freedom, or what seems to him to be a freedom, to do certain things. But the narrowness of the limits in which we are all confined may be quickly seen if we attempt to reverse the decisions of our strongest faculties. Strange as it is, people do not stop to think that their own faculties restrain them from certain actions. When subjected to analysis, nothing can be more obvious than the fact that every will is an effect, necessarily dependent upon adequate causes, and that the same causes must always produce the same will. "Man is free," says Lavater, "like the bird in the cage; he can move himself within certain limits."

As a product of nature, each human individual presents the agglutinated results of all the influences which have ever affected him, from the remotest ancestor down. The causes of the will are, therefore, chiefly the causes which have combined to produce the personality of the individual, and are often determined before he becomes a conscious entity. Thus we are all free to evolve whatever wills do not conflict with any of our desires or impulses, and the amount of freedom we possess with regard to a particular will, must depend upon the number and power of the opposing influences.

In view of these facts, is it not utterly impossible to render credible the fabled fall of man? And if this account is a myth, is not the whole system of orthodoxy also a human invention? If Adam never fell, we certainly have no need of any Redeemer. But what says the Church on this point? One Commentator remarks: "It is difficult to conceive how our first parents, being holy, could sin. But as we have the fact, it is not necessary to inquire into the philosophy beyond what is given." This well illustrates the spirit of blind faith so characteristic of theologians. They begin to study the Bible with the preconceived idea that it is a supernatural book, and when they meet a contradictory fact, they simply ignore it, or boldly assert that the Bible transcends science, and does not need to be reconciled with logic.

But such evasions will not silence the eager inquiries of the present generation. It will no longer suffice to say that the "Fall of Adam" is a "mystery" which God never intended us to understand. In fidelity to our deepest convictions we must admit that the story of Eden is simply an oriental fiction. In the foundation of orthodoxy it is only a lump of crumbling clay. It never has been, and never can be, reconciled with our only possible criterion of truth.

## CHAPTER III.

#### CHANGE OF HEART.

ONE theologian says: "The great majority of those who take the Bible as the rule of their faith, have always understood it to teach, that, since the fall, all men are wholly depraved—distitute of all holiness, and disposed only to sin. In this belief, they are sustained by many of the plainest declarations in the inspired volume."

This doctrine is clearly contradicted and disproved by the fact that all goodness, or holiness, proceeds from the brain, and that, other things being equal, the development of the brain determines the amount of goodness. Some have, to be sure, more than others; but nearly all persons have, by nature, a certain endowment of the superior faculties, and to assert that all men are inherently disposed only to sin is an exceedingly gross error.

It would probably be no exaggeration to say that all systems of supernatural religion originated in consequence of ignorance respecting the constitution of the mind. The ancients observed the weaknesses and follies of mankind, and as they were ignorant of the dependence of the mind upon the brain, it was quite natural for them to attribute all mental phenomena to the influence of spirits. Good thoughts were supposed to be suggested by good spirits, and evil thoughts by evil spirits. Something was evidently defective in human nature, and so it was supposed that man must have "fallen" from some previous state of perfection. It did not occur to them that perhaps the human race was slowly ascending, and had never before occupied so high a plane. Our savage progenitors simply reversed the order of development. If they had known a little more of nature, the idea of Adam and the Fall would never have been conceived.

But after the acceptance of this fiction, it became a matter of profound interest to discover some method of regaining that which was supposed to have been lost. As evil was held to be the offspring of a malignant spirit, it was therefore natural to think that only a good spirit could counteract it. This view of sin and its remedy is the popular one to-day throughout the world. Theologians still teach that human depravity emanates from Satan, and that only Divine Grace can "cleanse the heart from all unrighteousness, etc."

But what light does science throw upon this question? Simply that sin is the direct result of a diseased or imperfectly balanced brain; a purely natural cause, the natural and only thorough remedy for which is to develop and cultivate the superior cerebral centers so that they will be supreme in power, or to re-establish the health of the brain, as the case may require.

The so-called "change of heart" is nothing

more or less than an awakening to special activity of the superior brain centers, particularly Conscientiousness, Veneration, and Wonder. Its rationale is no more wonderful, no more supernatural, no more difficult to understand, than the arrows of Cupid, whose subtle power is daily manifested among the youth of our acquaintance. When any of the emotional centers, for the first time, or after a long period of dormancy, suddenly become aroused to great activity, the effect is perceptible in the manifestations of all the other faculties. When a young man is for the first time conscious of a deep, chivalrous, and unselfish love for a pure and noble girl, every thing around him seems changed. The whole world is brighter; the flowers are more fragrant, and the birds sing more sweetly. He never before so thoroughly appreciated music. He now has a pleasant and friendly greeting for every person he meets. He is conscious of a tenfold greater ambition than he ever felt before. In short, he has been "born again."

Much that he once loved he now hates, and many things he once hated he now loves. He feels new life welling up within him. He is physically stronger than formerly, and his mental perceptions are all sharpened. Now, this is no imaginary picture. It is something with which all are familiar, either by personal experience or by observation. But who thinks of attributing this form of "new birth" to the influence of any supernatural power? We all admit that a pure sexual love, "*la grande passion*," is simply natural. And if so, what evidence have we to suppose that the phenomena of religious regeneration are not also produced simply by natural causes? The Christian may answer that sexual love is something which spontaneously springs up in all minds, without any effort to elicit it, and that it more frequently needs to be restrained than encouraged; while religious sentiment is repugnant to the natural mind, and is the result only of a subjection of the carnal nature, and a yielding to the Will of God; all which is accomplished only through the assistance of Divine Grace, and is therefore a supernatural process. Of course, this sounds very plausible. And with such ideas of the mental constitution, it is doubtless quite natural for one who believes his "heart" has been "renewed," to insist that he "knows" his religion is no "cunningly devised fable." He tells us that he feels in his soul the comforting voice of the Holy Spirit bearing witness with his spirit that his sins are forgiven, and that he is now an heir to salvation. Moreover, his "heart" assures him that he *"can not be mistaken."*

But let us look for a moment below the surface here. Briefly stated, the difference between sexual love and the effects produced by the so-called "spiritual" faculties, consists simply in this, that Amativeness is a purely selfish faculty possessed by man in common with the lower animals, and is likely to be strongly developed because of the exceedingly numerous causes which lead to its excitation; while the faculties which produce religious sentiment are found in their greatest strength only in the human mind; are among the highest faculties possessed by man; are purely unselfish, and hence are not so likely to be predominant. It seems to be a law of mental development that the higher the organism, the more susceptible it is to variation. The violin is the most sensitive of all musical instruments, and for this reason it is capable of a greater variety of expression than any other. Thus the human brain is the most sensitive and complex of all mental instruments, especially as regards the coronal or sincipital centers, and hence is the most susceptible to modifying influences. As the lower animals occupy a lower and much simpler plane of development, they are exposed to a much more limited number of modifying influences, and consequently the individual members of each species present a much greater uniformity in appearance and in intelligence than is found in the human race. It is, therefore, evident that all the inferior propensities, common to man and the lower animals, such as Amativeness, Alimentiveness, Acquisitiveness, Secretiveness, Combativeness, Destructiveness, etc., are more frequently well developed than Conscientiousness, Benevolence, Veneration, Ideality, etc., simply because the climate, the food, the education, in short, all the influences which tend to produce and strengthen the basilar nature, are more abundant than the refined atmosphere of poetry, philosophy, justice, humility, and philanthropy.

It is, however, a great mistake to suppose that sexual love, or any other one of the lower propensities, is spontaneously active in every individual, and that it may always be aroused to activity by trivial circumstances. There are thousands of persons naturally so deficient in Amativeness, that the very thought of marriage is repugnant to them. Others never have any desire to accumulate wealth, and never learn to economize. The same is true of all the faculties. They are developed in all imaginable combinations. One individual "makes a hobby" of music, but greatly dislikes merchandising. Another is completely absorbed in literature, though detesting mathematics, while a third holds in utter disregard every thing that does not promote the interests of his religion. It is simply a question of cerebral development. Allow me to remark that whenever I speak of the effect of the brain upon character, I always mean to include the influence of quality, temperament, education, etc., as well as the condition of size. The size of the cerebral centers, however, is the primary point to be considered. Education may modify predominant tendencies, but it never wholly eradicates them. It is true that "just as the twig is bent the tree's inclined"; but still we can never convert an oak twig into a pine tree. For the convenience of the expression, at least, I shall continue to speak of size as the source of power in the brain. Thus, if a man inherits, or otherwise acquires an excessively large cerebellum, he is very susceptible to sexual love, perhaps bestows his affection upon some playmate when a mere child, and continues to love some one all his life. He can not recall a time when he did not feel that some one of the opposite sex was necessary to his happiness; that is, he can not recollect when he underwent any change. Another man can not recollect a time when he was not passionately fond of music. There never was any particular moment when the love for music became suddenly aroused in his mind. In short, he was born a "convert" to music, simply because of a peculiar cerebral organization. In like manner, a great many persons inherit a large endowment of Conscientiousness, Veneration, Wonder, Hope, and Benevolence, with deficient animal propensities, which prompts them even in early childhood to do what they believe to be right; to venerate superiors; readily to give ear and credence to all accounts of marvelous events; to cling to the ideas taught them concerning immortal life; and to practice charity, and all the other so-called Christian virtues. Such persons are frequently baptized in infancy, taught morality and trained to habits of religious devotion; literally nursed in the bosom of the Church, and while yet children, become members of a religious organization. In later years, when they are more matured, they anxiously ask themselves, "Am I converted?" "Have I really been 'born again'?" They apply to themselves the tests upon which they have been taught to rely in this matter, and they find that they have the evidence of the "new birth," although they can not recollect when the "change" took place. They love to do right, to worship, pray, etc., and as they have been taught that such feelings are not natural, and can come only from Divine Grace, they conclude that they have indeed been "regenerated," and that this "change" has been effected by a supernatural agency.

Now, to any one acquainted with the constitution of the mind, it is, of course, very plain that no miraculous "change" or spiritual birth ever occurs in such cases, but simply that certain physical conditions determine every phase of religious feeling. Sincere piety is never known to be manifested except by those persons who are endowed with a peculiar cerebral organization, and it is certain that no person not thus constituted can be truly pious. If "regeneration" is a supernatural process, why does it never take place in individuals who do not possess a peculiar development of the superior parts of the brain.

It is a popular belief that men of the vilest and most depraved character are often instantly converted, and become models of goodness and piety; but there could not be a greater delusion. It is not true that such individuals belong to the "most depraved" class. In every instance, they will be found to possess the cerebral centers of the moral sentiments just in proportion to the amount of morality or piety they feel after conversion. To this there never is, and never can be, an exception. In cases where men have led very wicked lives, and have suddenly embraced

Christianity, and become very pious, they will always be found to possess a large development of the centers in the base of the brain, combined with a large, or at least a fair, development of the "moral centers" also. Such combinations occur very frequently, and may be found in every church. Such are the individuals who generally "backslide" during the summer, and return again to the church at the annual winter "revivals." They also, when first converted, often need to pray with great assiduity and patience before they receive the "blessing," as it is called. It is quite an interesting psychological study to observe their efforts at the "mourners' bench," keeping in mind the peculiar conditions with which they believe it is necessary to comply in order to "obtain religion." The method is somewhat as follows: *First*, the seeker must become "convicted," which means that he must become profoundly impressed with a sense of his unworthiness and guilt. *Second*, he must have "faith"; that is, his intellect must be brought to believe that by renouncing all sympathy with sin, and by a total surrender to Christ, he will receive pardon, and his "heart" will be radically changed. *Third*, he must then resolve to give up every thing displeasing to God, and throw himself wholly and unreservedly upon Jesus as his Savior. The instant he makes this surrender, "in faith," he is to receive the "blessing," which is the token of his acceptance, and which will then constitute him a "child of God."

Let us now examine this process. *First*, it is necessary to be convicted of sin. The first step in this operation is through the intellect, which simply decides upon the fact of sin having been committed. This being presented to the whole faculties, a reversed action of Conscientiousness follows, producing the feeling called remorse. Here we perceive the natural cause of the supposed influence of the Holy Ghost in awakening "Godly sorrow for sin." And let me remind the reader that the intensity of remorse is always in proportion to the development of the cerebral center of Conscientiousness. *Second*, the penitent must have "faith" that Jesus is ready and willing to forgive and "bless" him. Now, as I have explained in the first chapter, "faith" is belief accompanied by the emotion of Wonder. In this case, there must be an intellectual conviction or assurance that there is a Divine Spirit hovering near, looking into the souls of men, and waiting for their permission to enter and take possession. Then this belief excites the faculty of Wonder, producing an emotion which is recognized as "faith." This explanation will account for the fact that "faith" is often used as a synonym for confidence or belief, and perhaps quite as often in the sense of an emotion. It should not be forgotten that the intensity of "faith" as an emotion, is always in exact proportion to the cerebral development of Wonder. *Third*, the act of "entire surrender," which is often very difficult, is simply the consent of all the faculties, a will, to yield completely to the wishes of Christ; and the powerful inhibitory emotion accompanying this action is produced by the great excitation of Veneration. The result of this complex mental operation, this "new birth," is thus simply an awakening to unusual activity of these higher faculties, with, at the same time, a subjection or suppressed activity of the lower propensities. The effect upon the mind, called by Methodists the "blessing," truly a very exalted and happy condition, is produced, *first*, by the relief afforded the faculty of Conscientiousness by the knowledge of having faithfully performed every known duty; *second*, by the tender, humble, submissive feeling caused by the excitation of Veneration; and *third*, by a kind of ecstasy produced by the faculty of Wonder.

Those who are acquainted with mesmerism will be struck by the great similarity of these two classes of phenomena. Religious trance and the mesmeric sleep are unquestionably identical as regards the fact of their mutual dependence upon a peculiar influence of certain activities in the brain, although of course the first links in the chain of causes producing this cerebral action may not be the same in both cases. It is a physico-psychological law that each propensity, when excited, has the power through the medium of the sympathetic nervous system to effect such changes in the action of the vital organs as will facilitate its gratification. For example, when Combativeness is aroused, and the feeling of anger is produced, the action of the vital organs is immediately accelerated. The heart beats faster, and the blood circulates more rapidly, thus preparing the body for a violent conflict, although it may be that no thought of a physical encounter has so much as entered the mind. The observation has been made thousands of times that men become almost superhumanly strong when very angry, although few understand the philosophy of it. When Alimentiveness is greatly excited, the appetite presumes, so to speak, that something is about to be eaten, and forthwith the necessary fluids are secreted for the first steps in the digestive process. Nearly every one has noticed the sensation of saliva flowing into the mouth at the mere sight of acid fruit. Vitativeness, or love of life, exerts a wonderful influence upon the vital action, and when strongly developed, often enables its possessor to conquer diseases to which persons differently constituted in this respect would very readily succumb. Of the vivifying and exhilarating effects of Amativeness I have already spoken. It would also be unnecessary to describe the well-known power of Hope to "lighten the heart." The faculties I have just named, together with a few others of the same character, are all invigorating, or exhilarating, in their normal effects, and may be denominated the exalting propensities. But there is another class which, from their inhibitory influence, may be called the depressing propensities. These are, chiefly, Veneration, Wonder, Imitation, Cautiousness, and Secretiveness. The former class, for the most part, belong peculiarly to the male sex, and constitute the executive, aggressive, or *positive* elements of character; while the inhibitory faculties are *negative*, and peculiarly feminine. The reader will, therefore, readily perceive that it is the especial province of the latter class to offset all undue manifestations of the positive faculties, in order to secure harmony in the operations of the whole mind. Thus, Veneration counteracts Self-Esteem; Imitation modifies Firmness; Cautiousness restrains Combativeness; Benevolence softens Destructiveness, etc. And as the exalting propensities impel the vital organs to act with great energy, the depressing faculties proportionately diminish the vital action. For example, when Cautiousness is greatly affected, the feeling we call fear is produced, and a great depression of the vital action immediately takes place. Digestion ceases, and the whole body is almost paralyzed. In fact, this depression has often been known to occur so suddenly, and with such a shock as to cause instant death. Again, many persons are affected by a chronic excitement of this faculty, often in utter ignorance of the cause, and finally die from its subtle effects. That is, they are frightened to death, although by imperceptible degrees. All are familiar with the shriveled face which artists give to the ideal miser. It always has a warped, mean look, and is never represented as bright and cheerful. Here we see the effects of Acquisitiveness and Secretiveness, with deficient Hope, Mirthfulness, etc.

Bearing these familiar facts in mind, the reader will be prepared to understand how Veneration and Wonder also exert a peculiar influence upon the vital functions. When excited in an ordinary degree, the emotions produced by these faculties are highly agreeable and healthful; but when aroused to a state of abnormal excitement, particularly in the case of individuals who are temperamentally very susceptible to such influences, they are capable of producing a variety of injurious effects, which, while presenting many features in common, are greatly modified according to circumstances. Among these phenomena may be enumerated religious trance, the "new birth," or "change of heart," mesmeric sleep, hypnotism, hysteria, hallucination, catalepsy, ecstasy, witchcraft, etc., etc. One noticeable circumstance attending all these manifestations, is the diminished circulation of the blood, evinced by coldness of the extremities, paleness of the face, etc. As the ancients frequently observed such symptoms accompanying mental excitement, of course it was but natural for them to conclude that the heart was the seat of the affections. And while modern science shows that the heart is the source of neither good nor evil, we see that good or evil emotions do affect the heart. However, in theology it seems to be the rule to reverse the order of facts.

The investigator of psychological phenomena who has ever attended a "religious revival," can not have failed to observe that the ministers, and others who assist the penitents at the "altar of prayer," urge upon them especially the necessity of two conditions; viz., "faith," and "entire surrender." Now, it is the intense effort of the seeker to make this complete "surrender," which directly and powerfully excites Veneration; while the belief or expectation that a supernatural change is about to take place in the mind, is peculiarly adapted to stimulate Wonder. From the circumstance that Veneration restrains the energy of the vital functions, giving to the whole mind a subdued, mellow tone, we can easily understand why persons habitually in this beatific condition should imagine themselves assisted by Divine Grace. The faculty of Wonder, although primarily excited by intellectual cognitions or beliefs, in its turn, together with Veneration, stimulates the intellect to a contemplation of the highest conceivable ideals, and in this manner does much to elevate the mind above the sphere of the lower propensities. But is there any thing supernatural in this?

I have already referred to the powerful influence of Cautiousness. It is well known that in ordinary dreams this faculty often incites the intellect to conjure up scenes of terror which are indescribably vivid and real to the imagination. Upon this principle then, why may not all the other depressing faculties exert a similar influence upon the intellect? And if in ordinary dreams at night, why not in a species of extraordinary dreams by day? That the cerebral center of Wonder, when unusually developed, together with certain temperamental combinations, is frequently the immediate source of visions, apparitions, and a great variety of strange impressions, can not admit of the slightest doubt, in view of the numerous observations made by Phrenologists. The curious reader can find descriptions of a great many such cases in the works of Gall, Spurzheim, and Combe. Indeed, all history abounds in instances of these phenomena. Shakespeare, who probably possessed a deeper intuitive perception of human nature than any other man who has ever lived, recognized not only the influence of cerebral action in creating illusions, but also the change in the circulation of the blood, which accompanies the trance state. As an example, note the following words between Hamlet and his mother:

> *Queen.*—This is the very coinage of your brain:
> This bodiless creation ecstasy
> Is very cunning in.
>
> *Hamlet.*—Ecstasy! my pulse,
> As yours, doth temperately keep time,
> And makes as excellent music."

Hamlet denies having any symptoms of trance, but we have too much evidence bearing on such cases to believe him. Besides, there are almost infinite phases of ecstasy, in many of which the changes in the heart's pulsations are barely perceptible.

Christians of nearly all sects point to frequent examples of what they are pleased to denominate miraculous cures in answer to prayer, etc. But if the faculty of Cautiousness can depress the life currents so as to cause death, why may not the exalting propensities produce equally marked results of an opposite character? In view of the numerous cures effected through mesmeric influence, why should we attribute any similar phenomena to forces outside of nature? There are numberless well authenticated cases of cutaneous excrescences being removed, and various other like effects, by simple faith in some foolish charm. The imagination wills the result, and forthwith the circulation of the blood to the affected part is either suspended, or increased, as the circumstances may require. The famous so-called miracle of the "Stigmata," said actually to occur in Roman Catholic countries, may easily be accounted for on this principle. It also appears probable that many of the alleged miracles of Christ may have had some real foundation in certain mesmeric phenomena, which, of course, eighteen hundred years ago, would have been greatly exaggerated, and explained only on the hypothesis of supernatural power.

But thus much is certain: no man can "enjoy religion," as the Methodists express it, unless he has well developed Veneration and Wonder. And for all believers in supernaturalism, whose brains are developed chiefly in the sincipital region, it is very easy to practice religious exercises; while those whose lower propensities are very greatly predominant never become sincerely devotional. Of course this fact is usually denied by supernaturalists, but it is nevertheless demonstrably true.

Some, however, are willing to concede that the Holy Spirit operates on the mind only through the medium of the brain, and only in harmony with certain fixed and unalterable cerebro-organic laws; but the moment this is admitted, it must be conceded also that there is no evidence of a supernatural agency in these phenomena. The majority of theologians teach that man is by nature entirely destitute of holiness, but science demonstrates that all persons inherit it in some degree, while very many are naturally endowed with a great deal.

At this point, it may be well to mention that the word *natural* may be construed to have two meanings which ought to be clearly defined. *First*, we often say a thing is natural if it is produced independently of any human effort. *Second*, we may use the word simply in the sense of that which is opposed to the supernatural, thus including every thing which is accomplished without the aid of the supernatural, whether it be through voluntary human effort, or through the spontaneous action of impersonal natural forces. It is in this latter sense that I use the word. Thus I say that the goodness in humanity is natural, because it is independent of the supernatural; and yet it often requires much personal effort to develop it.

The position of the Church, as is well

known, is, that any one can "experience religion," independently of any particular cerebral development. In fact, the whole idea of the culpability of those who reject Christianity, is based upon that error. But how inconsistent this is, when, at the same time, it is universally admitted that idiots can not be converted, and are not responsible for any of their acts! And now, how will Christians dispose of all the moral idiots in the world? In the face of millions of facts, they simply deny that such persons exist. But, I wish to ask, if all persons can become moral and religious, why is it that some never do? It will not suffice to answer that it is because they do not "choose" to do so. It is very obvious that they do not "choose" to do so. But *why* is their choice thus? If it is not because of their organizations, what other explanation can be given?

It is unnecessary to dwell longer upon this subject. The fact is incontrovertible that the brain makes the man, and there is not only no evidence to show that gods or demons have any part in the formation of character, but we have excellent proof that such is not the case. Christians ought to bear in mind that if we do not happen to know the cause of a phenomenon, it does not necessarily follow that a supernatural agency has produced it. And now that mental physiology has demonstrated the dependence of all moral sentiment upon the brain, they ought to be more modest in their use of the verb "to know." The great mass of mankind are both by nature and education (or the lack of it) illogical, and comparatively few persons appreciate the distinction between knowledge and belief. Various kinds of evidence may induce us to believe, but we can not know any thing except that which is demonstrable by fact. Phrenological facts prove that certain cerebral developments are necessary to the sincere expression of all the higher as well as all the lower qualities of mind, and hence, so far as we can know any thing in this world, we know that all mental manifestations are only natural.

## CHAPTER IV.

### THE PLAN OF SALVATION.

THE story of the curse pronounced upon the human race, and all the circumstances of the vicarious atonement, are so familiar that it will be unnecessary to repeat them here. We will, therefore, proceed at once to discuss the merits of the scheme for man's redemption.

*First*, then, of what benefit is this "Plan"? The Church must concede one of two things: It is either necessary to believe in Christ in order to escape an eternity of pain, or it is not necessary. If it is not absolutely necessary, what is the meaning of the declaration, "He that believeth not shall be damned"? If it is not always necessary, and if the heathen and other honest unbelievers may be saved, why preach the dogma of faith, or insist upon its importance? It is idle to say that it should be preached simply because the Almighty has ordered it. The question is, is there any thing reasonable in the command? Is not the very absurdity of it sufficient evidence that no God ever gave it? The Church replies: "It is necessary for all to believe who have heard the Word." The senselessness and injustice of this doctrine may be shown in the fact that *belief does not depend upon volition.* Circumstances, education, inherited or acquired prejudices, in short, the evidence presented to the intellect, is the sole cause of belief. No matter in what form the evidence is presented, belief can spring from nothing else. And as it is utterly impossible to believe a thing simply by willing to do so, to require a man to believe that which is opposed to his reason would violate every principle of equity.

Is it logical to suppose that a God of infinite love ever devised a scheme for the salvation of the human race, and then permitted circumstances to defeat the operation of the scheme in the case of the millions who have never even heard of it? Admitting that those will be saved who have never heard the Gospel, what is the difference, morally, between them and the honest skeptics who have heard and yet are wholly unable to believe? The Buddhist, for example, of course can not believe in Christianity if he has never heard of it. And, if simply hearing of a thing is enough to inspire confidence in it, why does not the Christian believe in Mohammedanism, or the Jew in Buddhism?. To the sincere Roman Catholic, the weight of evidence which has come to his mind seems to him to favor the Roman Church, and he can not resist this belief. Just the opposite is true of the Protestant. To the Humanitarian, who has examined all creeds, and found all forms of supernatural religion based upon ignorance of nature, the weight of evidence is, as a mountain to a pebble, in favor of the Cause of Humanity. He can not resist the force of the evidence presented to his mind against supernaturalism, and so he is driven to believe simply in nature. Now, could a being possessed of any justice or mercy punish one of his own children for an honest conviction? It must be conceded that circumstances control the belief of all individuals, and while Christians admit that their *God is the author of all circumstances*, they deny that he is the author of any man's belief or unbelief. This inconsistency grows out of the erroneous doctrine of free-agency. Every will, every belief, is a result of organization and environment, and if any God has created the mechanism of the human mind, he must be responsible for the working of that mechanism, in the same sense that a man is responsible for the striking of a clock, although he may not have touched it since he made it and set it in operation. *Qui facit per alium, facit per se.* Would the maker of the clock have a right to deny his responsibility for its striking, on the ground that the striking was produced solely by forces within the clock?

Surely not; for if he made the clock, he combined the forces which compelled it to strike, and he is therefore responsible for the action of those forces.

Many theologians of the present day admit that faith, in the sense of an intellectual conviction, does not depend upon volition, and that it is always determined by the evidence presented to the understanding; but they say the kind of faith necessary to salvation is a consent of the whole faculties to a life of purity, etc. However, this is only disguising the difficulty, and presenting it in another form. It is wholly unimportant how we define the word faith. No matter what that condition of mind may be, if it is a condition of the mind at all, or an act of the mind, it must result from organization and circumstances. Hence, if there is any God who is the author of the human mind and the circumstances of its development, he alone is responsible for every operation of that mind, whether it be faith and submission, or doubt and disobedience.

To the objection so frequently offered, that this doctrine involves an utter denial of all moral responsibility, and discourages wicked men from all efforts to reform, I would say, *non sequitur.* Science does not affirm that all men are destitute of moral restraining faculties, or that individuals can not improve themselves by exercising such controlling forces as they may possess; but simply that individual responsibility is to be estimated by individual restraining power. As to the responsibility of criminals under a civil code; of course society must protect itself whether men can control their passions or not. But the wants of society can not be compared with the conditions of an omnipotent Creator, because the latter would *need no protection.*

It is often said that "God made us and has a right to do with us as he pleases." To this we reply that might does not make right. If there is a God of infinite power, and he creates an immortal soul, knowing that it will suffer an eternity of pain, he can be nothing else than an infinite fiend. It can only shock the sympathies and confuse the intellect of an unwarped mind, to be told that such a being is infinitely kind, loving, and merciful. As to the doctrine that "the natural heart is averse to God," we freely admit that no unpolluted heart can love a God who would establish an institution for the endless perpetuation of suffering. "But," says the Christian apologist, "if these things are terrible, and incomprehensible to our finite minds, the Bible teaches them, and therefore they must be true nevertheless." To this we repeat, that for the very reason the Bible does teach these infamies, it must be simply a human invention.

However, admitting that any particular belief, or the acceptance of any particular creed, or the attainment of any particular mental condition whatsoever, is necessary to salvation, how is the mind to be guided to it? This is an important question to the honest unbeliever. If the condition is reached at all, it must necessarily be acquired in one of three ways. It must come either as a "gift of God," or by reason, or by accidental circumstances. Now let us briefly examine each of these methods:

*First*, if this "saving faith" is a "gift of God," and he purposely withholds it from certain men, could any thing more unjust be conceived than that he should then damn those men? If it is God's plan to inspire faith in the minds of all who are to be saved, is he not then responsible for the skepticism and consequent punishment of all disbelievers? Some Christians hold that faith may be obtained by prayer. But how is the sincere Infidel to pray when he has not even the slightest degree of confidence in prayer? To ask a confirmed Atheist to pray for faith is about as rational as to advise a drowning man to swim to the shore for a boat. There are thousands of noble men and women who have not faith enough even to begin to pray, and if orthodoxy is true, they must suffer eternally, or else it is not orthodox doctrine that belief in Christianity is essential to salvation.

There is no possibility here of evading a dilemma. If belief is an absolute requisite to salvation, then the millions of sincere disbelievers must suffer the most heinous injustice conceivable. Or, if no such condition is absolutely necessary, then the story of the atonement becomes a fable, and the plan of salvation a farce. What was the need that Christ should die to save the believing sinners if the disbelievers can be entitled to the same salvation? And if honest Infidels can not be saved the same as believers, then God is measurelessly unjust and cruel.

It is sometimes admitted that if a man should live a pure life, that is, exhibit the sinlessness of a Christian, without faith, there might be some hope of his salvation. But if it is conceded that simple morality, or honest devotion to the Religion of Humanity, can entitle a man to salvation, is not this a positive contradiction of every fundamental teaching of the Christian religion as distinguished from Atheistic or Humanitarian philosophy? If the skeptic can fare as well as the believer, of what value are Christ's words to Nicodemus: "Except a man be born again, he can not see the kingdom of God"? Why should a man be converted, or "born again," if he can be endowed with the elements of holiness at his natural birth? And that this is possible can no longer be denied. It is vain to say that lofty-minded Infidels are indebted to careful training in childhood, or Christian parentage, for their moral excellence. It is now conceded by the most eminent theologians, that all the moral principles of Christianity were taught and practiced by heathen philosophers who never heard of Christ or the Christian Bible. Hence, there can be no reason why men to-day can not attain the same development independently of Christian dogmas. But, granting, for the sake of argument, that the word belief, used in the Bible, does not necessarily mean belief at all, and that to avoid any reflection upon the justice of God, it may be interpreted to mean "good works," or purity of character; the question still remains, would there be any justice in God's consigning even a wicked man to everlasting pain, when the very cause of his depravity was an organization and an environment which emanated solely from God himself? If a man is inherently vile, and disposed only to evil, is he not an object of pity, rather than revenge? There are idiots in morality as well as idiots in intellect; and although society is justified in forcibly restraining such unfortunate persons, in self-defense, why should an omnipotent God, whom they can not harm, after creating them, inflict upon them a kind of punishment, which, in cutting off the possibility of reformation, could serve only to gratify the malignity of a demon?

*Second*, if faith is not an especial gift of God, and if it is proper that we should be guided by reason in the selection of a creed, ought we then to be cast into a "lake of eternal fire" for choosing a belief or disbelief which is in strict accordance with our reason? If the Roman Catholic Church should indeed be the "*Alleinseligmachende*," and our reason tells us it is but a corruption of the true fold of Christ, and that Protestantism expresses the true will of God, ought we to be punished for being Protestants? But suppose our reason assures us that neither Romanism nor Protestantism, nor any other form of supernaturalism is worthy of credence, ought we then to be held guilty because we still remain true to our convictions? Surely but one logical answer can be given to this question.

*Third*, if we do not receive our "saving faith" as an especial divine gift, and dare not trust to the voice of reason, there can be but one other way left; viz., by accident. That any soul could merit endless torment for not being aware of certain conditions which only accident or chance could make known, is an idea which of course needs no discussion. We are thus compelled to admit that no Deity could justly require human beings to observe any conditions whatsoever as necessary to salvation, since the possibility of our observing the conditions would rest with him alone, and he would therefore himself be responsible for every case of non-acceptance.

With regard to these obvious defects in the Scheme of Redemption, orthodoxy has given and can give but one reply; viz., "*There is no sincere Infidelity.*" And it is worthy of note that in the New Testament no special provision is ever mentioned for honest unbelief on the part of any who have heard the Gospel. However, nothing is easier demonstrated than the existence of millions who conscientiously reject the supernaturalism of the Bible in the face of every argument that can be presented in its defense. And linked with this fact the conviction must come to every candid and reflective mind, that the Plan of Salvation is consistent with neither the constitution of human nature, nor any logical conception of a just or merciful God.

## CHAPTER V.

### IS NATURE SELF-EXISTENT?

LA PLACE was once asked by Napoleon why he made no mention of God in his "Celestial Mechanism." The astronomer replied: *"Sire, je n' avais pas besoin de cette hypothèse."* [Sire, I had no need of this hypothesis.]

The idea of a God was first conceived in the efforts of primitive man to account for the existence and operations of the universe, and to this day it is only a hypothesis. If there is a personal Deity, he has never revealed himself as such. However, science does not assert that there is absolutely no God, but simply that there is none to us. There is no logical evidence of his existence, and until such evidence is produced, we have no reason to doubt that Nature includes the All.

But if there is a power superior to nature,

he must be an embodiment of matter and force, because force is inconceivable apart from matter. And he must either have created himself or have existed from eternity. Now, if we can believe in an eternally self-existent or self-created God, who is more wonderful than the universe, why can we not believe in an eternally self-existent universe? It is certainly just as reasonable to suppose that nature has the power to produce what we see, as to say that a personal being is the author of nature; and more reasonable, because we are confronted by the fact that the operations of nature do not spring from caprice or chance, but are in every case preceded by causes which do not vary from certain inexorable laws. Now, if there is a personality able to control nature, why does he never manifest himself except in accordance with these inflexible conditions? It is thought by many that the laws of nature can not properly be said to be invariable, because one law often interrupts the effects of another; as in the case of a storm, when the lightning destroys a growing tree. The tree grows according to one law, and the lightning checks its growth in accordance with another law. This is no contradiction, however, because it is clearly a general law of nature that the effects of one law may thus clash with those of another. What is meant by "invariableness of natural law," is this: Like causes always produce like effects. That is, in all cases where the causative conditions are the same, the effects will be the same, without exception. This is nature, and it is what is meant by the natural as opposed to the supernatural. Now, for example, it is a law of cerebral physiology that a man with a brain like that of Caligula, Vitellius, or Pope Alexander VI, is more prone to vice than to virtue. And if one instance can be shown where this rule is reversed, then we will admit that theology is not without a basis in fact. But until it can be demonstrated that like causes do not always produce like effects, we shall be forced to accept Nature herself as the ultimate mystery.

To say that God is a spirit, is simply giving a definition of which we can form no conception, and using a word which is valueless except as a symbol for our ignorance; and to say that God created the world from nothing, is the climax of absurdity. *Ex nihilo nihil fit* is an axiom which needs no proof. We are therefore driven to the conclusion that the universe, as an entirety, has existed from eternity, or, at least, that if there is a God, his hand is nowhere discernible in sublunary affairs. If we are to be happy and useful, it must be by our own exertions, and by the assistance of circumstances. The result is just the same to us whether we are produced by a Deity or by the inherent activities of impersonal matter, since we are subject to an inexorable government. Besides, if there is a Supreme Being, he does not need our homage. Suffering humanity deserves all our attention.

To a logical and unprejudiced mind, nothing can be clearer than that man has progressed just in the proportion that he has learned to rely upon his own efforts. Those of the nations and individuals who succeed in accomplishing much that is great and good, and who profess to trust in Providence, will always be found to act out in their real lives the policy of the Infidel. They follow the advice of Cromwell to his soldiers: "Trust in God, but keep your powder dry."

Belief in "special providences" is, from its very nature, necessarily antagonistic to reliance upon natural forces, and the world never will appreciate the importance of obeying the laws of nature until the popular ideas of divine superintendence over human effort are wholly discarded. Admitting that there is a Creator, if he never interposes to save us from the consequences of our mistakes, of what advantage is it for us to believe in him? It will not satisfy the thinkers of to-day to talk of "blessings," or wonderful cures in answer to prayer, etc. None of these things afford the slightest proof that theology is not a chimera. There are many things within the infinite domain of the natural which we do not understand, hence, occasional phenomena which we can not explain by any known process, furnish no evidence for the existence of forces outside of nature. The only method by which it would ever be possible to demonstrate the existence of a Deity, would be to bring forward a greater array of facts against the principle that "like causes always produce like effects," than we now possess in favor of that principle. It would be necessary to produce more instances of reversed natural laws than we now possess evidences of their invariableness. In other words, it would be necessary to observe a greater number of phenomena unaccompanied by discernible causes than we have already observed in connection with their causes. So long as the preponderance of evidence is indicative of a fixed natural order, all inexplicable phenomena which might appear to contradict this principle, should be regarded as within the domain of nature, although not explainable by any process with which we have as yet become acquainted. But, if the time should ever come when the exceptions to the rule are more numerous than the examples of it, then it will be proper for us to renounce the rule, and not until then.

It seems remarkably easy for the defenders of any one creed to detect the absurdities in every other, and hence there is scarcely a particle of evidence to be found to-day favoring the existence of a Supreme Being, which has not been condemned as worthless by theologians themselves, if we take their own admissions made from time to time. Thus the whole Bible is thrown away between the Jews and the Liberal Christians. The former reject the New Testament entirely, while the latter discard the Old, or at least hold such views of it that they might consistently reject it altogether. For example, Dr. Robert Collyer says the Old Testament is a "rotting tree." David Swing thinks it is a "poem." Another eminent divine looks upon it as a "picture," while still another says that the question of truth "as applied to any ancient book is simply nonsense."

In the same manner, the champions of theology differ respecting the evidences of a Deity to be drawn from the automatic or unconscious activities of the material world. The most profound class, of which we may take the celebrated anti-phrenologist, Sir William Hamilton, as a representative, freely concede that the phenomena of inorganic matter indicate nothing more than the blind mechanical march of cause and consequence; the necessary expression of an inexorable and impersonal absolute, which, so far from giving any support to the hypothesis of a Creator, would, on the contrary, ground even an argument against it. But orthodox philosophers usually, as is well known, assert that this very inflexibility, order, and precision, in the operations of the physical world, show the "handiwork" of a great personal architect.

So much for "spiritual discernment"! And how strange it is that Christians do not more readily detect the unsoundness of the methods by which their leaders arrive at such antagonistic conclusions!

However, while the most learned theists find no evidence of a God in the manifestations of inorganic matter, all are united in basing their faith especially upon the phenomena of mind. The psychical activities they suppose are but indirectly, or partially, and at most only temporarily, subject to material restrictions, and in no sense governed by such immutable laws as control the material world. In short, all orthodox Christians hold that the human mind may act independently of organism, and that it may be influenced to good through the operation of the "Holy Spirit," or poisoned by the machinations of "Satan," irrespective of any particular cerebral structure.

We can easily understand how such a view of the mental constitution was suggested to our primitive ancestors who knew nothing of the relations between mind and brain; but it is deplorable, to say the least, that such a misconception should still be popular throughout the world.

To-day, we know with as much certainty as we need to know any thing, that force is not independent of matter, and that the activities or manifestations of brain substance, which we call mind, are not only inseparable from the brain, but modified by every varying shade of development or susceptibility in the cerebral organization. All this is more than proved by Phrenology; hence it follows that *the laws of organic matter are as invariable as those of inorganic matter*, and that mental phenomena are but links in the eternal chain of cause and effect, which are as mechanically necessary as the expressions of the grossest substance. In view of this fact, then, can we wonder that the Church should still be hostile to the philosophy of Gall? Truly this conflict is one in which there can be no compromise. Either matter is self-existent and automatic or it is not. If it is self-existent, and if force is impossible apart from matter, then it must be conceded that the phenomena of mind are, after all, only the phenomena of matter, since mind is but an expression of organic matter, and subject to the same mechanical necessity as the inorganic world. And since the most scholarly theists admit that the phenomena of inorganic matter, *from their purely automatic or mechanical nature,* tend to refute the idea of a Deity, we have virtual authority from the Church herself, that *all phenomena, by whatsoever name,* not only afford no evidence in favor of a God, but, on the contrary, clearly point to his negation.

We may summarize the argument in the following propositions:

1. The most profound Christian metaphysicians concede that the phenomena of inorganic matter refute the hypothesis of a Creator.

2. Phrenology demonstrates that all phenomena have a purely material basis, and that the activities of organic matter, called mind, are, in point of mechanical necessity, virtually identical with those of the inorganic world.

3. Therefore, the greatest minds in the Church logically admit that *all phenomena* contradict the notion of a God.

But what of miracles? Very little indeed. A genuine miracle, that is, a violation of the order of nature, would, unquestionably, point to the existence of a Deity; but where did a miracle ever occur? From the preponderance of evidence we now possess demonstrative of Nature's sovereignty, we are compelled to account for every reputed miracle in one of two ways: First, nothing occurred at all. Or, second, if any thing really took place, it was a phenomenon depending upon some purely natural forces probably unknown to those who saw it. A suspended law of nature would be excellent evidence if such a thing could be substantiated;

but any thing so extraordinary as a miracle could not be proved by any thing short of another miracle; and, if we really saw one, we could never be certain that we recognized it. A miracle, to have any value, must be an interruption of an established order of nature; but the very evidence which would establish an order of nature would be fatal to the miracle. Only a God superior to nature could make a miracle possible, and nothing short of a genuine miracle could prove the existence of a God. Hence, to establish either, it is necessary first to prove the other, which leaves both absolutely destitute of any support.

## CHAPTER VI.

### THE DESIGN ARGUMENT.

THE next line of reasoning to which the theologian appeals, is the one based upon the apparent design exhibited throughout the world, and especially in the wonderful mechanism of man. This famous argument is exceedingly interesting to the logician, being, as it is, one of the most remarkable sophisms ever evolved from the human mind. Many of the leading Doctors of Divinity now see the weakness of it, and admit that the labored efforts of Paley and others in this direction can afford no satisfaction to any logical thinker, from the fact that the solution they give is more inexplicable than the problem. But while all genuine scholars readily perceive the shallowness of "Paleyism," the great mass of theists of all classes still suppose that it is unanswerable. To persons of superficial reflection, the wonderful adaptation of means to ends in the various objects of nature seems necessarily to point to a great designer outside of nature. For example, we are told that these adaptations could not have been produced by chance; that they could not have made themselves; in short, that they could have been produced only by an adequate cause, and that this cause must have been a personal intelligence. Now, no Materialist will assert that the fitness and order in nature have come by chance, or that they have not been produced by adequate causes. But we do say that there is *no logical evidence* to show that the causes of these adaptations are independent of certain unvarying laws, or that they have personality. The question is, is it true that adaptation, order, and harmony are *always and necessarily evidence of design*? Can it be stated as a first premise, that adaptation in an object always implies that it must have been designed and created? The teleological syllogism is substantially as follows:

1. All objects exhibiting adaptation must have been designed.
2. The objects in Nature exhibit adaptation.
3. Therefore, Nature must have been designed.

Now, a logical argument is a method of proving a certain statement by showing that it is contained or implied in some other statement the truth of which is *already admitted*. Thus we may say:

1. All men are mortal.
2. Thomas is a man.
3. Therefore Thomas is mortal.

Here the conclusion, "Thomas is mortal," is logical, because it will be granted that all men are mortal, and that Thomas is a man. The premises in a syllogism must always be admitted at the outset, or else they must be supported by a careful induction of facts. That is to say, they must be proved; otherwise the conclusions deduced from them would be worthless. But let us examine this first proposition. "All objects exhibiting adaptation must have been designed." Is this statement universally admitted? Is it sustained by any induction? Does it rest upon a universal observation and experience? Or is it merely an assumption? If we look at the mechanism of a watch, we readily and correctly infer that it was planned and constructed by a personal intelligence; in fact we know that it was, because we are *acquainted with its history*. But suppose we contemplate the sublime evolutions of the planetary systems, or the intricate and subtile machinery of the human body. Can we say that these were contrived by a person? Do we know that they were? Have we any logical evidence that they were? None whatever; simply from the fact that under any conceivable hypothesis regarding the origin of the universe, we must admit the existence of order and adaptation in *some form, which never were created or designed*, and which are equally as wonderful as any thing in nature, if not infinitely more so. For if we refuse to accept the universe with its activities as eternally self-existent, and imagine some great personal being as its author, we must admit that he would necessarily possess quite as much order and fitness as the universe, else he could not create it. Therefore, since it is thus clearly demonstrable that *some form of adaptation* can and does exist which is *no evidence of design*, it is obviously absurd to assume that *all* complex and harmonious objects of whose history we are ignorant must be the work of a designer. And yet this assumption is the essential foundation of the whole teleological argument.

Dr. Paley asserts that the Deity possesses the peculiar quality of self-sustenance, or self-sufficiency, wherein his nature differs from that of all other beings, and which renders it unnecessary that he should have had an antecedent.

But why might we not as easily say all this of *matter* ?

The chief difficulty in this subject is due to the fact that people will not stop to reflect that if there were a God, his organism (whether material or spiritual), if it could be examined, would necessarily display even more fitness, order, harmony, and adaptation, than are now to be found in nature. However, if it be objected to this that the fitness and order in God are *eternal*, and therefore *unlike* the transitory phenomena of nature, we reply, that while many of the adaptations in nature have indeed had a beginning and will soon cease to be, before the teleologist can show that the order and harmony in a God would be essentially different from the adaptation in the universe, he must prove that *matter itself* can not be self-existent, and eternally possessed of a fitness or adaptation to evolve the particular manifestations which we behold. Since matter is indestructible, it must be eternal; and if it is eternal, its properties or forces must also be eternal or self-existent. Hence, so far as we can logically determine, the universe, as an entirety, is impersonal, and contains within itself the causes of all phenomena. At all events, it is no solution whatever of the mystery of existence to say that nature has been created. For if nature is the work of a creator because it is complex and wonderful, then that creator must himself have been created, because he is wonderful. If twice two apples make four apples, twice two oranges must make four oranges. If it is logical to say of one organism whose history we do not know, that because it is wonderful in its construction, it must have been produced by a personality outside of it, then it must be equally logical to say the same of any and every other wonderful organism whose history we do not know. Now, it is certain that we do not know the complete history of the human species, and if we believe that there is a God, we must also confess our utter ignorance of his origin, so that whatever we assert *a posteriori* of one such unknown history, must be equally applicable to every other. Therefore, if man must have been produced by a personal Deity because the human mechanism exhibits a wonderful adaptation of means to ends, then that Deity must also have been produced by a creative personality external to him, for the reason that the organism of a God must be even more wonderful in its adaptation and harmony than that of man. And if God must have been created because he is wonderful, his author must also have had an antecedent still more wonderful, and so on, *ad infinitum*. Thus, wherever we dare to stop in this interminable series of creators, we find ourselves at the very point from which we started; viz., face to face with an eternally self-existent Absolute. And in the form of an anthropomorphic Deity, it presents a problem even more difficult and unsatisfactory than an uncreated impersonal universe. Since this is true, we perceive that before we can establish the major premise in the design argument, we must demonstrate the very idea which the whole syllogism itself is intended to prove; viz., that the universe is the work of a personal intelligence.

George Combe, although himself a theist, in speaking of Paley, Durham, and other defenders of the argument from design, makes the following unanswerable and sweeping criticism upon their method: "So when it is asserted by these writers that whatever shows marks of design must have had an intelligent author; and that the world shows marks of design, they virtually assert that the world had an intelligent author. But this is assuming that to be true, which the atheists deny, and which, in fact, is the very proposition that they themselves pretend to be establishing. In short, the attempt to ascertain in this way the being of God, is merely a tautological play of words; inasmuch as his being must be proved, before the premises can be laid down."

What more need be added? We have seen that order and adaptation either in the

form of a universe or in the form of a God,
must have existed from eternity, and that that
which has existed from eternity could not have
been designed. If there is a personal creator,
he must be an organism possessing an adaptation to create; and if he has existed from
eternity we must admit that the adaptation in
his organism never was designed. And if there
is no God, of course we must admit that the
order, adaptation, and harmony in nature never
were designed. These facts prove that the
adaptation in nature is in reality no evidence
whatever of an intelligent cause, and that the
whole design argument is without any logical
support.

The unfair methods by which theologians
usually try to evade this difficulty, may be well
illustrated by the reply once made by Dr. Lyman Beecher when asked by his students how
they should answer Infidels who told them the
argument from design proved too much. "They
assert," said the students, "that if every ap-

parent design must have had a designer, there may be twenty Gods." The Doctor replied: "Well, you tell them that if there is one God it will go hard with them, and if there are twenty it will go harder yet." Is it strange that Christian ministers are illogical after receiving such training? However, Joseph Cook, who relates this story, pretends to give a "scientific answer," a discussion of which the reader will find in the succeeding chapter.

Many persons who in some degree perceive the feebleness of the design argument, admit that the idea of an uncreated God is as difficult of comprehension as an uncreated universe, and then they ask, "if one of these problems is as great as the other, which we concede, what objection do you have to our uncreated God?" We reply that we object simply because there is no evidence that such a being exists. The ladder of design by which the theologian reaches God, extends through all infinity. If we take one step upon it, we must climb on and on forever. As it can bring us to no resting place, why should we begin such a fruitless journey? Supernaturalists ought not to insist that there is a God until they bring forward some evidence of his existence, and so long as there is no such evidence, they ought not to ask why we wish to dethrone the Deity. "But," they ask again, "if the adaptations in nature do not prove a designing cause, how were they produced? We answer, that although we can not trace the ultimate processes by which these results were effected, when we say that Nature produces them by a power within herself, we at least give quite as much of a real solution as those who ascribe all phenomena to an inconceivable personality outside of nature. The word God, the so-called "first cause" taught by theology, is only a sort of algebraic $x$ in the problem of the universe. The scientist accepts the difficulty at the outset, instead of simply removing it beyond his immediate sight. The explanation offered by theologians has been aptly compared to the folly of the ostrich with its head concealed in the sand. It is only a hoodwink. A "first cause" of nature outside of nature is a logical impossibility. The universe is simply an animated infinitude of matter; a self-contained circle of causes and effects. The theologians ought to remember that it devolves upon them to prove that there is something mightier than matter; not upon us to prove there is not. But while the rules of logic do not require us to prove our negative, we can, nevertheless, explain very much of the apparent design in nature. We can now account for a great deal which only a few years ago was regarded as utterly inexplicable. The great scientists are every day discovering more and more. Scarcely any eminent scholars now dispute the leading principles of Evolution and Natural Selection. With the slightest clue to these great laws, what shall we, with our limited knowledge of nature's history, presume to say may not have been effected by their influence during the eternity of the past? In imagination we anthropomorphize the absolute, and then suppose we have mastered the problem of the universe. We deify the subjective ego of man "projected into objectivity," and regard it as the source of all wisdom and the solution of all mystery, while we contemptuously look upon nature as a materialization of impotence. But do we really understand Nature? Have we unlocked so many of her secrets that we can say she must be under the dominion of a God? Our ignorance should teach us modesty as well as logic. Why should we presume to fix a limit to the properties of matter, when we have scarcely learned the alphabet of science? And here let me say of scientists, that they have as much right as any class of men, to theorize and speculate in regard to the unknown and the unknowable. But it is very unfair to make no distinction between their conflicting hypotheses and their numerous positive demonstrations, as our opponents are often disposed to do. No scientist holds that any speculation is strictly a part of science. We ask simply that what we offer may be accepted at its real value, whether it is fact or hypothesis.

It is also objected to our idea of the eternity of the universe, that we have "no personal observation of it." True, we have not; but has the theologian any personal observation of the eternal existence of a God? In the first chapter I have already shown that there is a radical difference between the two positions. Theology, with its anthropomorphic Deity, its book-revelation, its pretended miracles, etc., is not only unsupported by our experience, but is diametrically opposed to it. On the other hand, while we can not by personal experience prove the eternity of the universe, such an idea is quite in harmony with our experience. In the same manner, theologians object that Infidels reject Christ and yet admit the existence of Homer, Demosthenes, and other equally ancient characters. It is true we admit the existence of all ancient personages of whose lives we have credible history; but when history asserts events connected with their lives which are plainly opposed to reason and universal experience, we reject such statements just to the extent of their unreasonableness. Thus we do not deny that Christ may have existed as a man; but that he was a supernatural person history fails to prove.

Every principle of anthropomorphic theism involves contradictions. If God is a person, he must be restricted to the limits of an organism. Hence, to say that he is infinite in extent, is highly absurd. As well talk of an endless "yard-stick." If the Deity possesses organism and personality, these qualities can exist only as the result of environment, which of course precludes the idea of infinity. Again, if God possesses benevolence, justice, anger, designing intelligence, etc., such as are ascribed to him in the Bible, he can not be infinitely wise or powerful, because those attributes imply finiteness and imperfection. An omniscient being would not need to employ reason in acquiring knowledge. If he made any additions to his knowledge at all, he could not be omniscient. All the intellectual powers of which we can conceive imply limited knowledge, and the very words "infinite intelligence" involve an absurdity. "For," as Prof. Fiske has well said, "to represent the deity as a person who thinks, contrives, and legislates, is simply to represent him as a product of evolution. The definition of intelligence being 'the continuous adjustment of specialized inner relations to specialized outer relations,' it follows that to represent deity as intelligent is to surround deity with an environment, and thus to destroy its infinity and its self-existence."

As to the other human faculties, it would be clearly impossible to exercise any of the passions or sentiments apart from finite relations to an external world. How could an infinite God have compassion, or sympathy, unless he suffered? And if he suffered how could he be perfect? It is true the Church replies that God as Christ took upon himself the finite human nature also. This is equivalent to saying that a circle can be both round and triangular at the same time. Furthermore, if God were omnipotent, how could he become angry? Anger proceeds only from Combativeness and Destructiveness. These faculties were born of the peculiar difficulties, dangers, and noxious impediments which abound in this world, and their exercise is inconceivable apart from environment and limited power. How absurd, then, to speak of "Divine Wrath," as though Omnipotence would ever need to manifest the chief characteristics of the lion and tiger!

But if the theist admits the absurdity involved in the idea of an "infinite person," and accepts God as a being who acts only in harmony with fixed laws, and whose qualities are necessarily undefinable, incomprehensible, and unknowable, he then *virtually becomes an Atheist* in all the proper senses of that word. The

Agnostic, or Materialist, has no particular objection to the syllable God, if it is used merely as a symbol to represent the unanalyzable activities of the universe; but in such a sense the term is unnecessary. Hence we prefer to employ simply the words Universe and Nature. The former to include the All as an infinite entirety, and the latter, which, from its etymology, means that which is born, to represent the more immediate activities and expressions of the universe.

Thus, while rejecting an infinite personality, we do not deny the existence of an "All-upholding," "All-enfolding" Absolute, of which we can know only as we are related to it through the peculiarities of our organisms. We do not wish to destroy any thing that is true and useful. We desire merely that the world may be taught to recognize Nature as the only source of goodness and happiness; that the realities of life may be seen as they are, and that mankind may attain the highest and best development possible.

## CHAPTER VII.

### JOSEPH COOK'S "SCIENTIFIC THEISM."

OF all the fallacies in theological reasoning, some form of the "vicious circle," or circular syllogism, is without doubt the most common, as well as the most specious and subtle. Defined in general terms, it consists in proving the premises by the conclusion, and then the conclusion by the premises. In other words, assuming or stating within one of the premises, something, the truth of which could never be established, or which would never be admitted, until after the demonstration of the conclusion. We have just seen a remarkable example of this kind in the preceding chapter. The whole argument from design begs the question; but the most singular feature about it is, that the leading theologians, perceiving their error, now come forward with a new set of circular arguments, which are, if possible, even more sophistical than the old. Of the champions of "Scientific Theism," doubtless the most popular representative in the United States is Joseph Cook, of Boston. In his lecture entitled "Matthew Arnold's Views on Conscience," Mr. Cook presents what he calls the "scientific answer" to the obvious defect in Paley's reasoning. I quote *verbatim:*

"But the answer is this: That we can not have a dependent existence without an independent or a self-existent being to depend upon. All existence, to put the argument in syllogistic form, is either dependent or independent. You are sure of that? Yes. Well, if there is a dependent existence, there must be an independent; for there can not be dependence without something to depend upon, and an infinite series of links receding forever is an effect without a cause. Your axiom that every change must have an adequate cause is denied by the theory of an infinite series. You carry up your chain link after link, and there is nothing to hang the last link upon.

1. All possible existence is either dependent or independent.

2. If there is dependent existence, there must be independent existence, for there can not be dependence without dependence on something. An endless chain without a point of support is an effect without a cause; dependence without independence is a contradiction in terms.

3. I am a dependent existence.

4. Therefore there is independent existence. But independent existence is self-existence.

1. All possible being is either self-existent or not self-existent.

2. If there is being which is not self-existent, the principle that every change must have an adequate cause, requires that there should exist being that is self-existent.

3. I am a being that is not self-existent.

4. Therefore, there is being that is self-ex-

istent. So, too, with exact loyalty to self-evident truth, we may say:

1. All possible persons are either self-existent or not self-existent.

2. If there exist a person that is not self-existent, there must be a person that is self-existent.

3. I am a person not self-existent.

4. Therefore, there is a person who is self-existent. It is He."

The introductory remarks, and the first four of these propositions, are, without doubt, substantially correct; provided, however, that we construe the third proposition to mean that man is "dependent" upon the universe in a relative and not in an absolute sense. In the second argument, the first and second propositions are also logical; but the third, "I am a being that is not self-existent," like the third proposition in the first argument, is true only in the sense that man did not attain personality by an act of his own volition; or independently of certain reactions between his organism and its environments which were necessary to his development. The fourth proposition is admissible, provided Mr. Cook does not here attach to the word "being" the idea of organism or personality. Man is, of course, a "dependent" or contingent being, so far as regards the fact of his having become an organism without any exercise of his own will; or in the sense that he is an objective expression or manifestation of a certain force or tendency inherent in matter, which may be said to underlie his personality. Thus, *relatively*, his individual organism is "dependent" upon this subjective force, or combination of forces and environments in nature; but, regarded *absolutely*, he forms a part of the eternally self-existent entirety of the universe. As an effect, he bears the same relation to the universe that the leaf does to the tree. A leaf is, relatively, an expression of a process or function of the tree, and is dependent upon this function only for its form and individuality. But as an absolute existence, it is a part of the tree, and is as independent of any forces outside of the tree as the tree itself is. Or, if it be objected to this illustration that the tree is not self-sustaining, we may compare man at once to the tree. Relatively, that is, as a definite structure, the tree is dependent upon its environments, such as earth, air, water, and light; but absolutely, its particles are composed of material elements found in earth, air, etc., thus forming a part of the universe as a self-existent whole.

Let us now especially notice the second proposition in the third and last argument, viz.: "*If there exist a person that is not self-existent, there must be a person that is self-existent.*" As this is the pivot upon which the syllogism rests, if it can not be established as true, the whole argument must fall. Have we, then, any evidence that it is true? Does Mr. Cook offer any? Not the slightest. He simply *assumes* that nothing short of a divine Person could be an adequate cause of human personality. And this he does without any induction whatever to warrant such a notion. This proposition is only a subtle method of asserting that there is a Creator, because it is on all sides conceded that, in a relative sense, man is not self-existent; that is, not self-sustaining, or independent of his environments. But what is the whole syllogism intended to prove? Why, simply that there is a Creator. Could there be any greater sophistry than this?

To make the "vicious circle" still more apparent, let us re-construct Mr. Cook's argument, and express it in words which will perhaps admit of less ambiguity:

1. All *non-self-sustaining* persons are caused by a *Self-Sustaining Person*.

2. I am a *non-self-sustaining* person.

3. Therefore, I am caused by a *Self-Sustaining Person*; i. e., by a God.

Now, it will be clear to the reader that the first proposition here virtually contains an assertion that there is a personal God; because, as

I have already explained, all concede that man does not exist or sustain himself independently of certain conditions and environments external to his organism. It will be equally clear that the third proposition, or conclusion, contains the same assumption. Thus the whole argument is a circle.

I have stated that man is *relatively*, non-self-existent, though when regarded *absolutely*, as a part of the indestructible entirety of the material world, he is self-existent. As this distinction might afford some ground for cavil, I will say that in this case it is entirely unnecessary for us to attempt to indicate man's exact relation to the universe. For the sake of the argument, we will concede that man is in no sense self-existent, and that he is contingent or dependent upon a "some-what" external to himself. Now, can, or does, Mr. Cook prove that this "some-what" is a "Some-One"? Admitting the third proposition, "*I am a person not self-existent*," upon what authority does Mr.

Cook lay down the second proposition, "*If there exist a person that is not self-existent, there must be a person that is self-existent*"? How is it possible to establish this premise, without first establishing the fourth proposition, or conclusion, which is, substantially, the assertion that there is a God? Is there not here a positive violation of the rules of the syllogism, which require that the evidence supporting the premises must be gathered from external sources? Induction must precede deduction. We have no right to draw a particular conclusion from a general proposition unless the latter is already admitted or has been demonstrated. Mr. Cook's argument is about as logical as the following:

1. All possible leaves either grow by themselves, or upon trees, or something resembling trees.

2. If there exist a leaf that did not grow by itself, there must be a leaf that did grow by itself.

3. The oak leaf is one that did not grow by itself.

4. Therefore there is a leaf that did grow by itself.

The gratuitous assumption here in the second proposition, and the absurdity of the conclusion, are of course apparent to every one. But is not this a counterpart of Mr. Cook's reasoning? Now, we see that there are no leaves growing by themselves. Moreover, we can not conceive of a leaf that did not grow on a tree, or something like a tree, and we are certain that the tree is mother to the leaf, *though not itself a leaf.* Why then may not matter be the parent of all human personality without being a person itself? We see the organisms of nature, and we know that they exist; but as we have not seen any Person behind them, where does Mr. Cook obtain his facts to show that there must be self-existent supernatural Personality to account for man? All reasoning must begin by observation. Has

Mr. Cook ever observed any Person superior to Nature? Possibly in his dreams; surely nowhere else. But still he boldly asserts that the only adequate cause of human personality is Divine Personality. And this is his "scientific answer" to the acknowledged difficulty in the design argument.

We find similar assumptions repeated in nearly all of his arguments for the existence of a Deity. Take, for example, the following proposition: "Since we are woven by a power not ourselves, there is thought in the universe not our own." Now, how does Mr. Cook know that this power proceeds from a Thinker? Has he observed all the potencies in the universe which have combined to weave us? And if not, how can he describe them? It is a contradiction in terms to speak of Infinite Thought, because the word thought means only the working of a brain, and thus implies environment. There may be something pervading all matter which resembles thought or mind; but the idea that exactly that which we mean by these words can exist as a personality without a brain, conflicts with all our experience, and hence is wholly untenable.

May I quote still another argument?

"1. Every change must have an adequate cause.

2. My coming into existence as a mind, free-will, and conscience, was a change.

3. That change requires a cause adequate to account for the existence of mind, free-will, and conscience.

4. Involution must equal evolution.

5. Only mind, free-will. and conscience in the cause, therefore, are sufficient to account for mind, free-will, and conscience in the change.

6. The cause, therefore, possessed mind, free-will, and conscience.

7. The union of mind, free-will, and conscience in any being constitutes personality in that being.

8. The cause, therefore, which brought me

into existence as a mind, free-will, and conscience, was a person."

Here the first three propositions are correct, also the fourth, in the sense that the sum of all the influences which combine to produce a result shall be adequate to produce it. But it does not follow that a cause shall necessarily always possess exactly the same individuality as the effect. The tree, as we have seen, is adequate to produce the leaf, but it does not follow that the tree itself must be a leaf. Books are written by men; but it does not follow that a man is a book. A great many effects are produced by combinations of circumstances which are indeed adequate to produce them, and yet, as individualities, the effects are totally different from their causes. Mr. Cook's apparent idea of involution and evolution would make it necessary that every individual effect should have only an individual cause exactly similar in character, thus denying the potency of combined influences. It is this fallacious view of the principles of cause and effect which enables Mr. Cook to declare in the fifth proposition, that only mind, free-will, and conscience in a God, could produce mind, free-will, and conscience in man. Now, I ask again, what observation has Mr. Cook made of the force or forces which produced man, that he should make this assertion? If he does not know exactly who or what is the cause of the human mind, why should he assume that it could have been produced only by an antecedent mind external to the universe? Does he know the history of man? Or does he know the extent of the forces in nature? And yet Mr. Cook says: "If you will look at that list of propositions, you will find nothing taken for granted in them except that every change must have an adequate cause."

I appeal to the reader. Do not those propositions contain the assumption that only mind, free-will, and conscience in the cause of man, are sufficient to account for these qualities in man? And is not this something more than simply that "every change should have an adequate cause"? No one denies that man originated from an adequate cause; but this is not the only proposition "taken for granted" here by Mr. Cook. With his usual subtlety, he simply assumes that which he professes to demonstrate.

It matters not what form of argument is employed, it must forever be impossible to prove that nature is contingent, until it is first demonstrated that there exists a power superior to nature.

# CHAPTER VIII.

### THE CORRELATION ARGUMENT.

THE earlier theologians, especially those who held the doctrine of total depravity, were inclined to disbelieve that man possessed any instinctive reverence, or willingness to submit to a divine law, and they usually accounted for all religious manifestations by what they supposed to be the influence of the "Holy Spirit." But in our day the professed "scientific" defenders of orthodoxy come forward with the confident assertion that a tendency to worship is one of the inherent elements in the constitution of the mind, implanted there by the "Creator." And they argue that as there can not be a wing without air to match it, a fin without water, or an eye without light, so there must be a Deity as a necessary correlative to the mental faculty of Veneration. Some form of this argument is probably almost as old as human thought; but since the time of Dr. Gall it has been brought into greater prominence than ever before; and, in this country, within the past few years, Joseph Cook has been presenting it upon such a gorgeous background of rhetoric that among the orthodox it has popularly come to be regarded as transcendently invulnerable. However, Mr. Cook and his school do not usually refer to any special system of mental science as a basis for their reasoning, and, unlike certain religio-phrenological authors, they seldom directly speak of the faculty of Veneration as such. Yet they frequently mention facts for which they are indebted to Gall when it suits their convenience to do so. At other times they are careful not to indorse, as Mr. Cook says, "a pseudo phrenology"; but, unfortunately for the "scientific theists," their strongest tower for the defense of their hypothesis can be clearly shown to be built upon the most pseudo Phrenology imaginable. The argument may be formulated as follows:

1. Every natural faculty or instinct has a correlate.

2. The existence of a faculty or instinct proves the *conjoint existence of all the objects* to which it is adapted.

3. There is in the mind a faculty of Veneration which is adapted to a God.

4. Therefore, as a correlate to this faculty there must be a God.

The first proposition here is entirely correct. There is indeed an object of some kind, existing either outside of the mind, or simply as an intellectual conception, to match every inherent faculty or instinct. But in the second proposition, we have the usual "*petitio principii,*" begging the question, or assumption of that which would be admitted only after establishing the conclusion of the syllogism. This argument is intended to prove the existence of a Deity, but it would be necessary first to demonstrate his existence by some other means, before it could be laid down as a premise that the existence of Veneration proves the conjoint existence of *all* the objects to which it is adapted. Hence, as an argument it proves nothing.

The normal function of Veneration, as has already been explained, is simply to inspire the feeling of reverence, humility, and submissiveness in general. It makes a child respectful and polite to parents and all aged persons, or recognized superiors of any age or sex, and is thus a very necessary element in a harmonious organization. Where it is very deficient the individual will manifest only a feeble disposition to respect authority, and, if otherwise unfavorably endowed, will be likely to evince an unduly rebellious spirit. But, I repeat, this instinct has no necessary connection with any single object, and the idea that it bears a special relation to any particular god may be conclusively disproved by the fact that in many nations we see it exercised in the worship of imaginary deities the conceptions of which are regarded by the rest of the world with utter indifference, if not ridicule and contempt. Again, we observe that as fast as nations develop and become civilized, their gods are also subjected to various changes both as to character and number. But all deities, of whatsoever rank or quality, are revered by the same mental faculty, the activity of the same superior cerebral convolutions, from the rudest fetich, up to the "meek and lowly Jesus." And then there are savage tribes entirely destitute of any supernatural religion, or even fetichism, who, in common with the brutes, simply recognize the existence of natural beings or forces more powerful than themselves, and who know no higher god than their Chief. To him they submit with a devotion like that of a dog for his master, and yet the feeling of reverence they have for their Chief is a process of the same part of the brain through which is manifested the awe of the Jew for Jehovah, or the veneration of the Christian for Christ. In the case of these savages, as with the brutes, the manifestation of Veneration is induced by a very limited and feeble reflection, or act of reason, and the objects to which it is directed are only such as are perceived by the senses. The supernatural religionist, however, takes a step beyond the brute and the lowest savage, inasmuch as he extends the objects of his Veneration into the domain of the metaphysical, where, in educing the conception of an anthropomorphic God as an object, he clearly makes a mistake. The Materialist, or Humanitarian (who also possesses Veneration, and often in a great degree), advances a step still farther, and by a complete process of logical reasoning, discovers that all conceptional Deities are only reflections of human attributes, and thus demonstrates that the true objects of our highest love and devotion are not imaginary Gods, but the living and unborn of our fellow men.

The oft repeated insinuation that Infidels are shallow reasoners, and always devoid of reverence, is too obviously false to warrant any special discussion here. It is true that Voltaire had large Veneration, and believed in a God; but his theism was not the necessary result of this faculty. It was owing more to the limited opportunities presented in his day for studying the principles of nature. In Voltaire's time, the "design argument" was scarcely ever questioned, and it was almost as much as one could do to shake off the grosser forms of superstition. However, it is not to be denied that the activity of Veneration often predisposes the individual to believe in a Deity, but this is easily explained by the circumstance that the faculty is intensely gratified by the worship of an imaginary person able to create and control the universe. Belief in such an extraordinary being necessarily tends to excite the faculty to an unnatural degree, and in the case of religious fanatics, it often produces serious injuries to the health of both mind and body. But because a certain object is capable of affording the mind

intense pleasure, it does not logically follow that
that object is legitimate or healthful. And the
idea that any of the sentiments or propensities
should be able to distinguish or appreciate particular objects independently of the intellect, is
as irrational as to suppose we could perceive the
rings of Saturn or the stars in the nebula of
Orion without a telescope. There is no mental
faculty that is not capable of being exercised
with reference to a great number of objects.
Thus Individuality observes an infinite variety
of individual things; Eventuality remembers
numberless peculiar and disconnected events.
Benevolence is not satisfied with a single good
deed; the mother's Philoprogenitiveness, independently of her intellect, knows no distinction
between her own children and those of another;
Cautiousness sees no danger, although it may
prompt the intellect to seek it out; Hope
brightens every uncertainty of the future; Wonder is gratified by every mystery, while Vener-

ation bows to the aged, to the noble, and to kings and emperors, as well as to gods.

To illustrate the weakness of the correlation argument, let us imagine the following syllogism:

1. Every mental faculty has an object to match it.

2. The existence of a faculty proves the *conjoint existence of all the objects* to which it is adapted.

3. The faculty of Acquisitiveness is adapted to triangular, rectangular, and octagonal, as well as round silver dollars.

4. Therefore, there are angular as well as round silver dollars.

Thus, if the method of these modern Theists is as "scientific" as they represent it to be, we may demonstrate the existence of all imaginable sorts of coins concealed in the National Treasury. Now, of course, if our Government should issue coins of various shapes, the popular Acquisitiveness would be gratified by the possession of them, and would be adapted or related to them;

but as we have no other evidence that any coins of an angular shape are made, we do not infer their present existence from the simple fact that we possess a mental faculty which would be adapted to them if they were made. For the same reason, we can not logically infer the present existence of a God merely from the fact that we possess a faculty of Veneration which would be adapted to the worship of such a being if he did exist.

Veneration has sufficient legitimate objects within the realm of the natural; but let us admit, for the sake of argument, that its instinctive tendency is exclusively to worship a God. If this could by any possibility be shown to be true, what would it signify? Or suppose there were a subjective cognition in any form, relating to a God, would it logically follow that such an instinct must have been implanted in the mind by a personal Creator? Before this could be established would it not first be necessary to prove that man is really the work of a

Deity? If it can be shown that the universe has been created, then the conclusion is indeed irresistible that all the inherent activities of the human mind proceed from a God. But as the evidences are overwhelming that man is a product of nature, whose brain is simply a register of experiences reaching back through unimaginable aeons, the possession of an instinctive desire to worship *presupposes only the various natural influences* (whatever they may have been,) which have combined to produce it.

The impulse to worship a God, so far as any really existing faculty of the mind may be thus designated, as well as the belief in a God, has undoubtedly been acquired, and is a legacy from our probable ancestors of a million years ago. And although it is instinctive to-day, and antecedent to individual experience, it must nevertheless be the result of the experiences of our early progenitors, the effects of which, operating through inconceivable periods of time, have become stamped upon the cerebral cortex as intuitions. "In the course of ages," says B. F. Underwood, "states of mind produced by the outward world have become organized in the race in the form of tendencies. A father who has acquired the habit of drunkenness may transmit to his offspring the result of his experience in the form of an appetite for stimulants. There are islands having species of animals and birds possessing an instinctive fear of man, but which exhibited no fear of him when he first visited those islands. Man by his destructive agency has produced in these animals sensations which by repetition, and by the transmission of the results on the brain and nervous system through successive generations, have become condensed and fixed in the species as an instinct which, whenever man—who first produced the impression—appears, manifests itself in a very positive manner. So the shepherd dog and sporting dogs have characteristics which, although originally acquired, are now innate or instinctive. Thus that which is learned, whether from a personal teacher or by contact with nature, and is repeated through centuries, may produce states of mind which by heredity appear in the descendants in the form of aptitudes or predispositions."

Considered from any point of view, an inherent element of the mind presupposes only the causes which have combined to produce man. As it exists to-day, the faculty of Veneration, when acting within a normal sphere, is one of the noblest attributes of human nature, but it was doubtless born of ages of oppression and pain, during which the emotions of gratitude and admiration were almost constantly mingled with fear and dread of the unseen beings who were supposed to control human destiny. Moreover, human governments, as far back as we can trace them, have nearly always been monarchical, and in many instances the rulers were cruel despots, and the subjects slaves. If we could look back to the period when men first became gregarious, the history of human slavery alone would almost be sufficient to account for a faculty of Veneration. How few nations there have been even within modern times, who have not bowed with admiration and reverence before the splendors of an imperial throne, or crouched and cringed in fear at the feet of a haughty king!

That the psychological basis of man's religious nature is an evolution from a condition like that of the lower animals, can no longer be reasonably doubted; nor is it less easy of demonstration that wild men exist to-day who have scarcely passed the boundary line between brute and man. And yet it is a popular belief, and one taught in nearly all orthodox pulpits, that there are no nations or tribes of men so low that they have not some idea of a Deity. But we have abundant testimony from such unimpeachable authorities as Darwin, Büchner, Lubbock, the Missionary Moffat, and a host of others, that there have been and still exist many such tribes. For example, the Bechuanas, the Arafuras, the Kafirs, etc. [See pp. 264–268, Büchner's "*Kraft und Stoff*," Leipsic, 1876. Also the article Bechuanas, in the Ency. Brit.] There can not be any ground for doubt on this point. These savages have evidently never even tried to discover any explanation of nature's mysteries. It is said that some of them are so incapable of appreciating novelty, that the sight of a strange ship produces in their minds no other visible effect than to elicit a momentary glance, after which they trudge along as indifferently as though they had seen merely a passing cloud. Is it strange that such beings should never have made an effort to account for their origin? Would it not be remarkable if they had? Like the uncertain steps of a little child learning to walk, the first attempts of primitive man to explain the phenomena by which he was surrounded, were feeble and crude, and it was but natural that his first thought should have been to invest the forces of nature with his own qualities, and give them personality. Thus, the first idea of a God was originated by a superficial operation of an embryonic Causality, and not from any instinctive sentiment. Then, after the dawn of this intellectual conception, we can easily understand how it affected the emotional nature. As the objects of our faculties are perceived only by the intellect, a simple belief in an object would have the same effect in developing a sentiment whether the object really existed or not. If there were really a God, his attributes would be apprehended only by the intellect, and hence if the attributes now supposed to belong to a God are only the qualities of human nature thrown out upon the objective world and contemplated as an illusion, the effect is the same upon the feelings as though these attributes really had an objective existence in a personal divinity; just as we may be moved to tears at a play when we know that the sorrows of the actors are only feigned.

With these facts before us it is certainly impossible to infer the existence of a Deity from the operation of any mental faculty. "But," objects the supernaturalist, "it is surely unreasonable to believe that we have been brought into existence endowed with instincts which mock us, and with hopes which can lead only to the most cruel disappointments." To this it may be replied that our lives here are full of disappointments. Nature is far from perfect. Pain and destruction are interwoven with the very constitution of terrestrial life, and it is impossible to reconcile any instance of human misery with infinite goodness and benevolence. "Eternal justice is a mockery, and compensation is a myth." Our utmost ingenuity can suggest no optimistic hypothesis which will conceal the fact of immorality in the government of this world. And if it is admitted that evil does exist at all, what logical reason have we to infer that on this very account some supreme being will compensate us after death? So far from there being any likelihood that a merciful God has instituted evil with a design of ultimate benevolence, the fact that so much sin and sorrow do exist renders it extremely unlikely that there is a benevolent God. But in any event, we may say with Prof. Fiske: "If there exist a personal creator of the universe who is infinitely intelligent and powerful, he can not be infinitely good; and if, on the other hand, he be infinite in goodness, then he must be lamentably finite in power or in intelligence."

Thus, to assert that God is infinitely benevolent, is equivalent to saying either that evil does not exist at all, or that God is not infinite in power. But as evil does exist, we must admit that there is no God, or else that he is finite either in goodness or power. We can choose here from three views. First, if we admit that there is no God, of course we need not hope for exemption from suffering. Second, if we accept the belief that there is a God who is finite in goodness, we can not with confidence rely upon him to compensate us for our misfortunes. Or, lastly, if we believe in an infinitely good although finitely powerful God, we can not consistently expect him to save us from disappointments. Now, whatever may be the real moral government of the world, it is evident that we are subject to some pain and disappointment. And if we are permitted to suffer any disappointment, how shall we logically say that we may not be disappointed as to the existence of a Deity?

It is objected that many Phrenologists advocate the "correlation argument," and that the teachings of "True Phrenology" are certainly favorable to it. I think that in the frequent definitions I have given of the faculties of Hope, Wonder, and Veneration, in this work, I have clearly shown that the teachings of Scientific Phrenology not only do not support any theistical vagaries, but, on the contrary, illustrate their groundlessness. As to the Phrenologists, it is true that some of them have not only inferred the existence of a God from the existence of the faculty of Veneration, but have also constructed some very plausible arguments in defense of this belief. But it should be remembered that the phrenological fathers, especially Gall, Spurzheim, and Combe, formed their ideas while modern Scientific Materialism was still in its infancy; besides, as I have already said of Voltaire, with limited opportunities and encouragements, they could not well be expected to divest their minds of every vestige of superstition. However, they never advanced those inferences with the assurance manifested by more modern writers. In concluding some remarks on this subject, in his "System of Phrenology," Combe was logical enough to make the following statement: "As, however, Veneration has likewise objects on earth, this argument can not be regarded as conclusive." Again, in his "Lectures," he says: "This argument has, of course, only the force of an analogy."

However, in this discussion it matters but little whether any phrenological authors accept the correlation argument or not. The only question for us to decide is, is it true? If it can be proven to be untenable, the mere assertion of any one to the contrary will not in the least change the fact. It should not be expected that all Phrenologists will exactly agree in their methods of interpreting details when we consider that this science is, as yet, comparatively new. It is only after any science is completed, and becomes firmly established, that we can reasonably expect its teachers to display perfect unanimity in their views. Moreover, there is scarcely any philosophical system which does not afford some opportunities for men to gratify their prejudices and selfish interests, either in a peculiar interpretation of its principles or in the application of them to the affairs of life. But here allow me to say, that as to the *facts* of Phrenology, its teachers have always substantially agreed, and it has been only in regard to certain inferences from those facts that they have differed. Thus, all Phrenologists admit that the faculty of Veneration in the minds of Christians is gratified by the worship of a supposed God.

But any inference from this fact as to the existence of a God, is, on the part of a Phrenologist, purely an act of his own mind, and entirely independent of Phrenology *per se*. Hence, Phrenology can not justly be held responsible for any such inferences until it is first proven that they are logical and inevitable deductions from its true principles.

It has been objected also, that if Phrenologists do not agree among themselves, they should not demand unanimity of belief among theologians. To this we answer that the cases are by no means analogous. Science is systematized knowledge, and it should not be expected that men shall agree upon a science any farther than the extent of their knowledge. Besides, it is not a principle with scientists that an erroneous opinion, if sincere, involves moral obliquity or guilt. But the religion of the Bible, so far as it differs from the beautiful Humanitarianism taught by the Infidel philosophers of every age, is chiefly a matter of belief, or faith, and since theologians declare that unbelief is a crime, and that "Infidels have no rights which the Church is bound to respect," we hold that they should at least decide which is the true Bible, and which is the true Church. They surely ought to be able to agree among themselves as to whether the Catholic Church is the "Spouse of Christ," or the "Harlot of Rome."

Christians pretend that the duties of their religion are so plain that "a way-faring man, though a fool, need not err therein." If this is to be believed, the inquiry suggests itself, in what condition is the mental organization of Roman Catholic and Protestant theologians? Now, scientists, we repeat, do not teach that any honest opinion or belief can involve criminality, since belief does not depend upon volition. Right beliefs and opinions are truly desirable, because they promote happiness; while false opinions are proportionately undesirable, because they are harmful. But, since both true and false ideas may be entertained conscientiously, it can not justly be asserted that they involve, when sincere, either morality or immorality. This being true, it follows that there is no imperative reason why scientists should exactly agree in the amount of their knowledge. But it is certainly unreasonable for theologians dogmatically to insist upon the performance of certain acts of faith, under penalty of endless torment, when they can not decide among themselves as to what constitutes these necessary duties. They ought to demonstrate the credibility of their doctrines, or at least the possibility of discovering the essentials of their creeds by agreeing among themselves, before they demand that we shall agree with them. In order to disguise this palpable inconsistency, Protestants are accustomed to refer to the harmony of belief among the "Evangelical Churches," while the Papists exultingly point to the unity in the "Church of Rome." But where is the harmony between Romanism and

Protestantism? It can not be denied that they are as incompatible as light and darkness.

In view of all these conflicts of opinion, there is obviously but one proper course to pursue; namely, let every individual freely express his sincere convictions, and then by comparing the thought of the world, it may be possible to educe the truth.

# CHAPTER IX.

### THE LOGIC OF JESUITISM.

THIS chapter will be devoted to a brief examination of the peculiar evidences upon which we are expected to embrace the dogmas of Roman Catholicism. I quote from a recent work which is used as a text-book in Catholic institutions, published under the *imprimatur* of Cardinal McCloskey, entitled "Evidences of Religion," by Louis Jouin, Priest of the Society of Jesus. On page 205 is the following:

"But it should be observed that, although in the present controversy we use the writings of the New Testament, we are not, as yet, considering them as divinely inspired, but only as the faithful records of the teachings and actions of the apostles. The inspiration of the writings of the New Testament can not be proved by historical criticism; it rests solely on the authority of the true Church. This remark suffices to set aside one of the chief arguments employed by Protestants against us, viz., that we fall into the sophism called by logicians *the vicious circle*. For, say they, you prove the Church from Scripture, and then Scripture from the Church. By no means. We prove the existence of the Church and her attributes from the New Testament, considered as a faithful historical record of what Christ and His apostles taught; then, having thus established the authority of the Church as a divinely appointed teacher, we learn from her that the Scriptures are inspired. Surely no flaw can be found in this line of argument."

To the careful reader, a very serious flaw can be found here. So far from giving a satisfactory explanation of the difficulty in question, Mr. Jouin simply disguises it by expanding the circle in which he reasons, thus rendering his claims more plausible, though none the less fallacious. To make the real significance of his propositions appear more distinctly, let us slightly abbreviate them. Instead of "We prove the existence of the Church and her attributes from the New Testament considered as a faithful historical record, etc.," let us substitute the following:

*The New Testament, considered simply as an authentic history, proves that the Church is a divinely appointed teacher. Then the teaching of the Church proves that this history is also divine.*

I do not think any one can say that this construction expresses any thing not contained in the quotation above, and I believe every reader will see at a glance that Mr. Jouin means to say the *divine attribute* of the Church as an *appointed teacher*, may be proved from the New Testament without considering the latter inspired. That is, he assumes merely from a historical point of view, that the writings of the New Testament are *authentic* and *sufficiently authoritative* to establish the divine attribute of the Church. This is one side of the circle.

And now the question arises, How is it possible to establish a *divine or inspired* Church by any evidence contained in an uninspired book? Is it true that the infallible authority of God could be conferred upon the Church simply by ordinary historians? In other words, could the voluntary statements of ordinary men regarding so important a matter be accepted as infallible or authoritative? Surely there could not be a more untenable position. Moreover, it would be absurd to say that any Catholic theologian ever does attempt to prove the divinity of the Church from the New Testament writings unless he first believes that they are inspired. But supposing that a sincere Romanist could by any possibility divest his mind of the belief in biblical inspiration, could he prove from the New Testament, considered simply as a profane history, that Jesus Christ possessed any authority from God to establish a Church? Unless it is first conceded that the Gospel narratives are divinely inspired, how would it be possible to demonstrate the truth of the alleged supernatural character of Christ? If he was not God, of course it would be only an assumption to say that he had any authority to found a Church; hence, the very first and most important point to be decided is that of his divinity. If the "Immaculate Conception" ever occurred, we must believe the most wonderful miracle ever recorded. But as this story is so preposterous, does it not need to be supported by the most unimpeachable testimony; nay, the most positive demonstration? Would the sworn testimony of a thousand persons be taken as proof of such a thing in the present day? Could any testimony short of an assertion by a divinely inspired writer, be accepted as unmistakable evidence of any thing so at variance with all experience and observation? Assuredly not. Even Mr. Jouin, on page 315 of the book in question, makes the following significant admission in regard to the Bible: "There are contained in it many mysteries surpassing the limits of the human intellect, which can be credible only when it is known that God really inspired the sacred penman who stated them." Now, if any thing in the Bible surpasses the human intellect, and can be credible only when known to be stated by an inspired writer, is not this very story of Christ's miraculous birth a case in point?

With reference to the means of distinguishing the true Church, on page 204, Mr. Jouin says, "we have to consult the records left us by the apostles and disciples of our Lord, if we want to establish its identity; forasmuch as its foundation is an historical fact, it can be proved by historical monuments alone."

Now, is not this a virtual admission that the New Testament contains the only "historical monuments" which really establish the authority of the Church? There is surely no so-called profane history sufficiently reliable to verify the Christian traditions. It can not be shown that any contemporaneous profane writer ever testified to the supernatural character of Christ. The oft quoted passage in some copies of Josephus, is, by the most eminent theologians, decided to be a forgery. The most ancient manuscripts do not contain it, and it was evidently interpolated by some of the early Fathers, who, by their own confession, were so thoroughly imbued with the spirit of Jesuitism that they regarded it as no sin to practice any deception which would aid in spreading their faith. However, suppose Josephus had made any mention of Christ's miracles, would it prove that they really occurred? The question before us is in regard to demonstration and authority; not mere tradition. And, admitting, for the sake of argument, that Josephus, Tacitus, Pliny, or any other non-apostolic writers, did refer to Christ, their accounts furnish no demonstration of his divinity.

And now, is there any other kind of collateral evidence sufficient to prove the authority of the Church? To prove any miracle whatsoever, would require a kind of demonstration as remarkable as the miracle itself. But it is unnecessary to dwell upon this point. The Romanists do not pretend to rely upon evidence outside of the Bible. On the contrary, they distinctly assert that they "prove the existence of the Church and her attributes from the New Testament, considered as a faithful historical record." And yet they declare that this record can not be established either as *genuine or authentic*, except by the dogmatic voice of the Church. Mr. Jouin, page 311, says that "the authenticity of a book must be shown by the uniform testimony of all the generations up to the very time when this book was written. Now, this testimony is given by the Church alone, as regards the New Testament; for, though some pagan authors mention some of the Gospels, and allude to some parts of the other sacred writings, they never testify to the genuineness and authenticity of the same in the form in which we have them now. Even early Catholic writers do not agree in these statements: more than one of the books actually contained both in Catholic and Protestant Bibles were by some considered doubtful. It was the Catholic Church alone that determined the canon of Holy Writ; on her authority were the apocryphal Gospels, and other writings attributed to the apostles, separated from those which are genuine."

We have now reached the other side of the circle. It will be remembered that Mr. Jouin first assumed the "faithfulness" (another word for authenticity,) of the New Testament records, in order to prove the authority of the Church, and here is his admission that the "faithfulness," or genuineness and authenticity, that is, historical value (to say nothing of the inspiration,) of the New Testament, depends solely upon the decision of the Church. It is a notorious fact that the canonical books were selected from numerous conflicting writings which were current within the first three centuries, and since it is admitted that the testimony necessary to prove their authenticity "is given by the Church alone," and that "It was the Catholic Church alone that determined the canon of Holy Writ, etc.," how can those writings be "considered" as a "faithful historical record," except on the sole authority of the Church? No theologian denies that the books of the New Testament were attested, if not selected, by an ecclesiastical vote. Thus the Romanists establish the inspiration or "divine" authority of this "record" by the voice of the Church, and then prove the inspiration or "divine" authority of the Church from this "record."

However, to explain this obvious inconsistency, they assert that reliable evidence may be adduced from non-ecclesiastical sources for the truth of *certain portions* of the New Testament canon which establish the divinity of the Church. But this is only a feeble makeshift, for there is in reality no such external evidence whatever that can be regarded as conclusive. Indeed all of the testimony given not only by the Pagan writers, but also by the early Fathers, is of such questionable character that many of the most learned Protestant theologians reject it, taking the ground that the Gospels must rest entirely upon their intrinsic merits. Besides, as I have already shown, according to the admission of the Romish Church, no historical criticism could be applied to any of the Gospel statements without regarding them as uninspired, which would reduce them to the character of profane history, and thus strip them of the only quality which could ever constitute them unimpeachable and authoritative title-deeds of the Church.

It will not suffice to say that because the canonical writings were generally regarded as authentic in the second century, and publicly read in the churches, they must be true; for it is admitted on all sides that as late as the beginning of the third century a great number of spurious gospels also were in circulation, and held by many to share equal authority with the books of the canon. And, although it can not be proved by historical criticism that the canonical books were written by the men whose names they bear, or that their accuracy was not disputed in the first and second centuries, we may grant, for the sake of argument, that the genuineness and authenticity of those writings were never called into question. But would such a fact alone render them authoritative? If a mere belief in a marvelous story is sufficient to give it authority, how can we logically reject any of the superstitions of the world? But what was the character of the times when the canonical Gospels were first accepted? Let me answer by quoting from the well-known Christian historian Mosheim: "For not long after Christ's ascension into heaven, several histories of his life and doctrines, full of pious frauds and fabulous wonders, were composed by persons whose intentions, perhaps, were not bad, but whose writings discovered the greatest superstition and ignorance. Nor was this all. Productions appeared which were imposed upon the world by fraudulent men as the writings of the holy apostles." And instead of growing better with the further spread of Christianity, the cloud of moral and intellectual gloom only settled deeper. Of the fourth century, Mosheim says: "The interest of virtue and true religion suffered yet more grievously by the monstrous errors that were almost universally adopted in this century, and became a source of immeasurable calamities and mischiefs in the succeeding ages. The first of these maxims was that it was an act of virtue to deceive and lie when by that means the interest of the Church might be promoted. The second equally horrible wrong was the production of an incredible number of ridiculous fables, fictitious prodigies, and pious frauds, to the unspeakable detriment of that glorious cause in which they were employed. And it may be frankly confessed that the greatest men and most eminent saints of this century were more or less tainted with the infection of the corrupt principle."

Scores of Christian authorities might be cited to show that in the early history of this religion it was common to forge whole books and palm them off as authentic. In the article "Bible," in the ninth edition of the Ency. Brit., the Rev. W. Robertson Smith says:

"All the earliest external evidence points to the conclusion that the synoptical gospels are non-apostolic digests of spoken and written apostolic tradition, and that the earlier material in orderly form took place only gradually in many ways. . . . All our knowledge of the period that lies between the apostles and the great teachers of the old Catholic Church towards the close of the second century, is fragmentary. . . . The analysis of the New Testament is the resurrection of early parties in the Church, each pursuing its own tendency by the aid of literary fiction."

What more need be added to this damaging testimony from honest men who believe in the divinity of the Bible themselves? However, we wish to do no injustice to the Romish Church, and while we do not accuse its defenders of *professing* to prove the Bible wholly by the Church, and *vice versa*, we hold that, according to their admissions, all the real *authority* possessed by either *is* derived from the other. Their exact teaching is that certain portions of the canonical writings are supported by sufficient historical evidence, aside from their inspiration, to establish the divinity and infallibility of the Church, and just here is the real fallacy. To evolve a "divinely appointed" Church from a non-divine book, would be producing an effect without an adequate cause. It would be a display in the effect, of an absolute quality which it is admitted was not in any sense contained in the cause. If there were no divine stamp or seal upon the canonical gospels they could not bestow a divine stamp or seal upon the Church. For example, if we ask for the *authority* of Christ's alleged promise to Peter recorded in Matt. xvi., 16–19, the answer can not be that the record is divinely inspired, and therefore infallibly true, but simply that it was *believed* to be true by many of the early Christians, each party of which was "pursuing its own tendency by the aid of literary fiction."

Again, the Church boldly assumes that as she is in *possession* of her seat at Rome, and has maintained her claim to the custody of the Bible for eighteen centuries, it devolves upon Infidels to prove that she was *not* founded by divine authority. But, I repeat (and it can scarcely be repeated too often), that in this matter it is the duty of the Church to establish her affirmative. If the mere fact that the Papacy has existed so many centuries is to be taken as evidence of her authority, what other false and pernicious institution of long standing might not be defended on the same ground? If the "Cause of Christ" is to be supported by such shameless sophistry as this, it must indeed be pitiably weak.

As is well known, Catholics assert that

Protestants have no means of proving the truth of the Bible. Mr. Jouin says: "We require the infallible teaching of the Church to know that the Bible is the word of God. Had we not her infallible testimony we could not know that there is a Bible, etc." Again, "If, therefore, the authority of the Church is not trustworthy, there is no means of proving that we have at present the genuine word of God. . . Were this authority wanting, there would be no means of knowing what Christ has revealed, and thus his mission on earth would be frustrated."

The theologians in the Romish Church are, without question, as scholarly as those of any other denomination, and if there were any arguments available to Protestants to prove the divinity of the Bible, the Romanists would certainly be acquainted with them. But, on this point, they say that Protestants have no better arguments to prove the Bible than the Turks have to prove the Koran;—an idea with which

Infidels perfectly agree, for it is certainly true. The only essential difference betwen the Koran and the Bible, is, that the latter contains more good literature than the former. But the fact that the Bible is the best book of its kind does not by any means establish its divinity.

In a former chapter, I endeavored to show that between the Liberal Christians and the Jewish theologians the authority of the entire Bible is rejected. And in these remarks upon Roman Catholicism, I wish to submit the fact that according to the testimony of Christian theologians there is no evidence to prove either a divine Bible or a divine Church. Romanists ridicule the efforts of Protestants to prove the authority of the Bible, and the Protestants hold in contempt the pretentions to authority made by the Church of Rome. Hence, as each refutes the other, we may be sure that the claims of both are worthless.

## CHAPTER X.

### POPULAR OBJECTIONS TO INFIDELITY.

IT is frequently asserted that Freethinkers manifest quite as much illiberality and aggressiveness as the Christians in whom they so strongly condemn these qualities. Nothing, however, could be farther from the truth. Is it "illiberal" to struggle for liberty? Is it "aggressive" to strike in self-defense? It will be said, perhaps, that the Church no longer persecutes. True, her faggots have gone to ashes; her thumb-screws have rusted; her racks are worm-eaten, and her blood-besmirched hands are now too feeble to wield the sword. But from pulpit and press, by tongue and pen, the venom of her enmity has never ceased to flow. In the past, Christians always persecuted in exact proportion to their power, and they do the same to-day. With the mass of the orthodox people, Infidelity is still a synonym for immorality and crime. A disbeliever in God and the inspiration of the Bible, is regarded *a priori*, as one who knows no law but his own evil heart; one who is devoid of both honor and reason; a wretch who would pollute the innocence of youth; a creature to be shunned as a "moral leper." Christians are taught that the fear of God is not only the "beginning of wisdom," but also the basis of all moral principle; and with such a distorted view of human nature, how can they logically regard the Atheist in any other light than that of an enemy to all that is good? But should we be called "illiberal" because we cry out against this injustice? Are we "aggressive" because we desire to be recognized for the manhood and womanhood we possess irrespective of creed? "The liberty of one man ends only where that of another begins." But does the Infidel enjoy such a liberty? Do Christians admit that he has a right to his unbelief? How can they admit it when they teach that he thereby not only loses his own soul, but by his influence drags others with him to perdition? What says the Romish Church as to the rights of Infidels? In her Papal Encyclicals, and in all her official utterances, she breathes the most deadly hatred to the principles of religious tolerance, and denounces every form of heresy as punishable crime. Therefore, we deny that we should be called "aggressive," so long as our rights are thus trampled under the heel of ignorance and superstition.

Moreover, if we do enjoy a comparative freedom to-day, we think also of the coming generations to whom we owe a sacred duty. The splendid liberties of the American nation are still threatened by oath-bound zealots of foreign birth and bias, who, in the name of Jesus, would but too gladly betray our all-protecting flag, and above the stars and stripes erect the bloody symbol of the cross. Until this danger is averted; until Infidels are allowed to testify in all courts of justice; until they are no longer regarded as disqualified for holding positions in the Government; until the money they pay into the public treasury is no longer plundered for the maintenance of superstition; until they are allowed to spend seven-sevenths of their time as they choose; until they are no longer looked upon as criminals before God and the Church; in a word, until they are recognized for their merits simply as men and women, the cry of "Illiberal Liberalism" should be repeated no more.

And here let me say that by the term Church, we mean only her false and pernicious dogmas; not the generous, trusting people who believe them. It is not against men and women that we contend, but against the superstition they have been taught, and which makes them cling to the follies and errors of the world's childhood, rather than the glorious certainties offered by the science of to-day. As Christians define Infidelity, they are themselves the only real Infidels, for their creeds lead them away from the great truths of Nature, away from a knowledge of the only means by which we can attain our highest and truest development. This is their misfortune more than their fault, and it is only their mistakes that we oppose.

It is also charged against us, that if we had the power once possessed by the Church, we would persecute Christians, and endeavor to extirpate them with fire and sword, exactly as they used to deal with our predecessors. This may be answered in a single sentence. We do not hold that any honest belief, however absurd or harmful, can involve guilt; hence we could have no motive for oppressing those who simply differed from us in opinion. The Church, on the contrary, teaches that unbelief is a sin, and thus renders intolerance and persecution inevitable, just to the extent that her dogmas are sincerely believed, and logically carried into effect. It is therefore clear that the two cases are in no sense parallel.

There should be no difficulty in understanding our position in this matter. We do not quarrel with the Church. The Church quarrels with us. If a peaceful citizen is awakened in the night by the hand of a burglar at his throat, is it "persecution" for him to resist such an attack and to expel the intruder? Moreover, if, on the following day, he takes measures to prevent the recurrence of such an outrage, should he be called "intolerant"? To what depths of puerile quibbling Superstition descends!

No; we are not aggressive. Let the Church *guarantee us our liberties and our rights*, and we will no longer oppose her. When she is able to do this she will have abandoned her unjust dogmas and all the features which make her hateful in the eyes of every lover of true liberty.

As to the comparison some seek to draw between the Freethinkers of to-day and the Pagan Romans who persecuted the early Christians, it simply illustrates the paucity of magnanimity and good sense which characterizes many of these would-be shepherds of human kind. What have modern Infidels to do with the superstitions of ancient Rome? Should we be expected to advocate all the vices of antiquity simply because we are not Christians? While Pagan Rome was in her highest glory the Hottentots were not Christians either. Does it therefore follow that Tyndall and Darwin, Huxley and Haeckel, and Bradlaugh and Ingersol, are Hottentots? We have no more sympathy with the unjust persecutions of Christians by the Pagans of old, than we have with the cruelties and crimes of medieval or modern Christianity. Let those who would know where we stand read our books, and study our lives, not superficially, but fairly and carefully, and they will see that it is we who have been the persecuted, and that we only ask for justice.

Another objection is, that we are so prejudiced against the Bible, that we do not examine it with sincere motives, and hence remain in ignorance of it. In other words, that we investigate only one side. Exactly the reverse of this is true. In renouncing supernaturalism, we part with much that is dear to us, as well as much that we instinctively abhor. While we rejoice at the emancipation of the human race from the infamous horror of eternal punishment, we are deeply pained by the conviction that there is much wrong in this world which no God can ever make right. Our religion of Nature demands much greater self-denial than that of the Supernatural, and representative Infidels who were once in the Church, in the majority of cases, relinquish their belief in God and the inspiration of the Bible, with much sadness and reluctance. They are driven to Infidelity in the very face of their prejudices. On the other hand, Christians believe exactly that with which they most strongly sympathize, and which they have not the courage to disbelieve. How unjust, then, under these circumstances, to impeach the Freethinker's judgment! It is the Christian who studies only one side. No Infidel was ever known to burn a book of "Christian Evidences"; but where are the Christian families who admit Infidel literature into their homes?

As regards the ignorance and narrowness of Freethinkers, we have no fears as to the result of a comparison between our leading minds and any of the defenders of the Bible. But, admitting that the best scholars in our ranks are usually deficient in Veneration, and are coldly intellectual; this is only an argument in favor of their views regarding supernaturalism. The diversity of creeds shows that mere sentiment is incapable of discovering truth, and as it is clearly the office of reason to guide the feelings, we must certainly conclude that those individuals who possess more intellect than sentiment are best fitted to perceive the truth without prejudice. To obtain the highest results in any particular department of mind, we must take a specialist in that department. This is a principle universally recognized and followed in everyday life, as regards commerce, mechanics, art, literature, music, etc., etc. Thus, within the province of mere reverence, and trusting faith, for extravagance we give the palm to theologians. But as regards *that which is*, and that which *may be known*—in this vast field scientists are the specialists, and the greatest of these specialists are Infidels.

To the charge of blasphemy, profanity, etc., I would say, that as we do not believe in the reality of any God, our strictures upon orthodoxy can not be said necessarily to spring from any inherent vulgarity, or lack of true reverence. And as to our accepting remuneration for our books and lectures, why should men not be paid for sound philosophy as well as for sound wheat or corn? To be sure, we sometimes make mistakes, but then we have never professed to be infallible or divinely inspired.

American Liberals have even been accused of wishing to encourage the dissemination of obscene literature. The sea has bounds, but the slough from which Superstition draws its missiles, seems to have none. This most unkind thrust has been dealt in consequence simply of certain perhaps overzealous, though honest, efforts to avert the evils and abuses growing out of a legislative system which is believed by many to be unconstitutional, and likely to pave the way for a restriction of the purest literature of Infidelity. Our leaders, foreseeing the difficulties in the way of adjusting any thing so intricate, have, it is true, advocated somewhat different and conflicting schemes with regard to this matter, but they have disagreed only as to the most legal policy to be pursued for the protection of the legitimate literature of Freethought. And the idea that any class of representative Liberals are in favor of promoting licentiousness, is simply absurd. Indeed, one reason why we oppose the Bible is because it contains numerous passages totally unfit to be read by any man or woman, much less a child; expressions and narratives extremely coarse without the merit of teaching any profitable lesson. And yet this vulgarity is said to be the Holy Word of an omnipresent, omniscient, and omnipotent God!

This leads me to mention the objection that Infidels are, as a rule, morally angular, and fragmentary, both in their heads and in their philosophies. I freely admit that they are to-day in some cases fragmentary as to their moral endowments, especially, however, as regards the illiterate ones; but I deny that this angularity is the result of their Infidelity. Their Infidelity is due rather to their angularity. For what is any infidelity, or heresy? Simply unfaithfulness, disloyalty, rebellion. All those who rebel against any form of government which in childhood they were taught to revere, must of necessity do so in opposition to the faculty of Veneration. Thus it is obvious that the less one possesses of the conservative, restraining faculties, the more easily he becomes a rebel or an infidel to that which his reason condemns.

On the other hand, the profoundly conscientious and reverential man, who sincerely regards unbelief as a sin, of course instinctively antagonizes every skeptical thought, and is thus likely to remain a slave to the religion learned at his mother's knee.

But let us trace the history of an immoral Infidel. For example, here is a young man who has been thoroughly instructed in the dogmas of Christianity, and in his youthful ignorance he believes they are true. But he has very strong animal propensities, with very deficient Veneration, Wonder, Conscientiousness, and Approbativeness. He soon develops an immoral character, and, while believing it to be a sin, he recklessly reads an Infidel book, discovers that there is no logical ground for belief in supernaturalism, and avows himself a Freethinker. Having never learned from his orthodox teachers his obligations to humanity, or the punishments Nature inflicts for the violation of her laws, with the one thought in his mind that there is no God, no hereafter, no retribution, he foolishly plunges deeper into vice than before. Christians then cry, "Behold the fruits of Infidelity!" But, in truth, the chief causes of this individual's wickedness were determined before he was born, and it was his indifference to what he erroneously believed to be his duty which enabled him to throw off the restraints of orthodoxy. As his only incentives to morality were interwoven with his ideas of allegiance to a capricious Deity, in giving up the belief in the Deity, he naturally loosened his moral restraints also. This is indeed the experience of many professed Freethinkers, but the fault lies neither with them nor with Freethought. It lies with the Bible, whose false and impracticable doctrines lead parents to disregard the laws of heredity, and to look with contempt upon all facts regarding the dependence of the moral faculties upon cerebral organization. If Infidels are immoral, it is because they have immoral brains, and not because

Infidel philosophy gives them any sanction to vice.

However, it is unfair to judge Liberalism by those individuals whose only training has been under the influence of theology, and who are very ignorant of the principles of Nature which they profess to believe. Humanitarianism imposes greater restraints, holds up loftier ideals, and leads to a higher development than any creed of the Bible. No mere negationist can be called a representative Liberal, but it is true that the pioneers in any great heresy or reform are generally more destructive than constructive, more aggressive and iconoclastic than reverent and conservative. If they were not, they could never withstand the opposition which is always encountered by those who labor to uproot error and dethrone tyranny. Look at the great rebels of history. Were they not all angular? There is always more or less temporary looseness in morals during the transition from one religious system to another, and it is inevitable, from the fact that every creed makes itself the basis of right conduct. When Christianity was in its infancy, Pagan writers complained that its influence was evil, because it destroyed the old incentives to virtue; but after it became established, and the forces in human nature found opportunity to assert themselves, the new system gathered to itself the majority of the best people in the world.

It can not be said that the leaders of the Protestant Reformation taught a morality less pure than that of the Romish Church, and yet it is a matter of history, especially as regards France, that that great heresy led to much temporary immorality and vice. And whenever this was observed by the Romish clergy, they invariably cited it as a proof of the essential wickedness of the Protestant religion. To-day, the doctrines of Liberalism are producing effects somewhat similar to those of early Protestantism, and no one should imagine that the moral defects of any professed Freethinkers are either warranted by the principles of Freethought, or necessarily produced by their application. To test the pure fruit of Liberalism, it is, I repeat, very unfair to pluck from trees grown in orthodox clay. Our Infidel philosophy has thus far been denied opportunity. Let those who oppose it at least examine its principles before denouncing it.

The foregoing paragraph calls to mind the seeming fondness of the average pulpit orator for dwelling upon the French Revolution as an instance of the terrible effects of unrestricted Infidelity. To persons at all acquainted with history, or with the principles of human nature, it would seem almost a waste of time to reply to such caviling; but as the orthodox armory contains no other kind of weapons, we may, perhaps, be justified in briefly noticing this spurt of spleen. Our answer is simply this: The French masses, prior to the period in question, had been nursed at the bosom of Romish Superstition, and were no more prepared to embrace the principles and privileges of Freethought than the eyes of a new born babe would be to meet the noon-day sun. But show us an instance where the teachings of Infidel leaders have been permitted to take root in virgin soil, and have afterwards budded and blossomed in the light of scientific Humanitarianism, and we will agree to be judged by the results. These remarks will also apply to the cases of those Infidels who have recanted upon their death-beds. There have, doubtless, been some Freethinkers, who, dying in their dotage, were unable to resist the impressions formed during their first childhood; but as to the Sunday School stories regarding the last hours of Paine, Voltaire, and other really representative Infidels, they have been repeatedly shown to be slanders born of the envy and impotence of the decaying creeds.

Another charge is, that Infidelity has never contributed any thing for the advancement of human happiness. Exactly the opposite of this is the fact. Some degree or kind of infidelity has contributed all that the world enjoys to-day. It is only by a species of heresy or disloyalty that any old error can be superseded by that which is newer and better. And as to supernatural religion, the only true symbol of orthodoxy is the starving and freezing monk in his cell. Whenever a man goes out into the world and works for humanity he is on the road to heresy. The truth is, the so-called Christian civilization of the nineteenth century is simply the offspring of heterodox influences which the dogmas of Christianity have been powerless to withstand. "Extinguished theologians," says Huxley, "lie about the cradle of every science as the strangled snakes beside that of Hercules." The spirit of orthodoxy has always been opposed to freedom and progress, and yet whenever a great reform is effected, Christians immediately assert that it is due to the Bible. For example, look back to the persecutions for witchcraft in Europe and our own New England, when hundreds of thousands of innocent people were put to death in the most cruel manner on the authority of the Bible. Such pillars of orthodoxy as John Wesley and Richard Baxter were among the foremost to encourage this monstrous wrong, but the first to raise their voices against it were Infidels like Voltaire and Hobbes, who trusted to reason rather than the vagaries of a deluded priesthood.

Christianity now claims the credit of having also abolished American slavery; and this in the face of the fact that the Bible sanctions slavery and polygamy in the most unequivocal language. In the Southern States, the clergy defended slavery on the authority of the Bible, and thirty years ago there was scarcely a pulpit in the North in which a man could protest against it. It was only upon the broad field of Rationalism that men could consistently oppose the plain teachings of the Bible in this matter, and hence Infidels were among the first and most zealous Abolitionists.

Civilization and morality have their foundation in experience and science. The fact that the Christian religion is popular in all of the most civilized countries, is no proof that it is the cause of their civilization. Alcohol and tobacco are also used in greatest abundance by the so-called Christian nations, but no one thinks of ascribing the enlightenment of the world to those articles. Again, what shall be said of the fact that these "Christian nations" are the most skeptical? All of the greatest leaders in scientific thought, the intellectual giants of the world, to-day, are Infidels. The only proper way to decide this question is to take the nations who have been influenced by Christianity without science, and compare them with the nations who have had both Christianity and science. For example, contrast Italy, Spain, Mexico, and Abyssinia, with Germany, France, England, and America. It is absurd to say that the degradation in Catholic countries has resulted from a perversion of true Christianity. The Romanists of all lands have had every doctrine instilled into them which distinguishes the Christian religion from Infidel philosophy; and the only points in which they have essentially differed from the most advanced nations, have been in matters of science and morality which Infidels have always been the first to defend. Nor will it suffice to attribute the superior enlightenment of Protestant countries to the fact that in them the masses read the Bible for themselves. Was the religion of John Calvin or John Knox less hostile to freedom of thought than that of Romanism? Does history afford a more horrid picture of fanaticism, bigotry, and persecution, than that of Bible-reading Scotland in the seventeenth century? Whence came the printing press, the sewing machine, the loom, the steamship, and the telegraph? From theology? Has the Bible contributed a single idea of value to the sciences of astronomy, geology, mathematics, chemistry, physiology, medicine, etc., which, in a thousand ways, promote the happiness of mankind? The whole marrow of supernatural religion is contempt for this world and all the achievements of man, while science is the friend of all that is good, beautiful, and true.

Lastly, it is said that Materialism destroys the immortality of the soul, robs man of his highest glory, and lowers him to an equality with the brutes. To this we can reply that if death does terminate our individual existence, neither Materialism nor Materialists should be blamed for it. If there is a hereafter, it is a fact in nature which no form of belief or unbelief can set aside. And if there is none, a mere belief in it would not make it true. "But," says the Christian, "you take away our hope in a future life, a hope which lightens our sorrows, and lifts us above all the grief and gloom of this unhappy world." Granting that this is true, ought we to suppress an important fact simply because some will temporarily suffer in consequence? The knife of the surgeon makes us shudder, and yet are we not often indebted to it for our lives? If there is no evidence to warrant us in expecting a life beyond the grave, will it not be best for the millions of our posterity to know the truth and learn to face it bravely?

As for me, I want no hoodwink upon my head or my heart, and I hold that in order to be truly noble men and women in this world, we must learn to accept the inevitable with courage and philosophic dignity. To do this it is not necessary to have less of true manhood or womanhood. And here I will say that, in my judgment, as broad intellectual culture, as much cheerfulness, tender sympathy, and unselfish devotion to moral principle as I have ever found, I have found among Materialists.

However, if any logical evidence for continued existence under favorable conditions can be produced, all true and sensible men and women in the ranks of Infidelity will welcome it. As to the Spiritualists, although I am not of them, I am with them in sympathy for their

Liberalism. I wish to thank them for the great work they have done in the cause of liberty and progress, and I cheerfully testify to the sincerity of their leaders, and to the unmistakable genuineness of many of the singular phenomena which form the basis of their philosophy. These phenomena are now attracting the attention of many learned scientists, and justly too, for they can no longer be concealed or ignored. Any thing which affects the cherished beliefs of millions of people should receive an impartial and thorough examination. The same scientists, both Christian and Materialistic, who have denounced all Spiritualistic phenomena as frauds, and disdained to examine them, have, in many cases, I am sorry to say, also ignored the facts of Phrenology. Now, whether our Spiritualistic friends succeed in proving immortality or not, I hope that none of us will ever forget to be true Liberals. Let us never scorn the most trivial fact in nature if it can throw any light upon the great problems of human happiness. Let us learn all we can.

If a future existence is ever demonstrated to be true, the credit will be due to science, not unreasoning faith.  And if at death we should end our only life, I say with Ingersoll: "Next to eternal joy, next to being forever with those we love and those who have loved us, next to that, is to be wrapt in the dreamless drapery of eternal peace.  Next to eternal life is eternal sleep.  Upon the shadowy shore of death the sea of trouble casts no wave.  Eyes that have been curtained by the everlasting dark, will never know again the burning touch of tears.  Lips touched by eternal silence will never speak again the broken words of grief.  Hearts of dust do not break.  The dead do not weep.  Within the tomb no veiled and weeping sorrow sits, and in the rayless gloom is crouched no shuddering fear."

## CHAPTER XI.

### OUR SUBSTITUTE FOR CHRISTIANITY.

IT is customary for Christians to point with pride to the beautiful moral precepts of the Bible, and then to turn indignantly upon Infidels with the question, "What can you give us in the place of this book?" In reply, I would ask, when have we ever proposed to destroy it? Have we ever declared that the Bible should be burned, or that the human mind should be thrown into chaos as to the duties and responsibilities of life? On the contrary, we accept all pretended Revelations for all they are worth, as monuments of the world's early thought, and especially do we wish to preserve and cherish all the good they contain. But theologians have no right to define the Bible or Christianity as the origin and source of all the principles of virtue, and then to charge us with the desire to sweep it all away. The moral beauties of the Christian religion were not born of any creed, and belong to no one nation. They were all taught by people who lived before the Christian era, and were largely interwoven with nearly all of the ancient superstitions. On *a priori* grounds alone we should be justified in regarding this as highly probable, for we have overwhelming phrenological evidence to-day that the impulses to morality were developed by the experiences of the primitive races, and hence that they must have been registered in the brain thousands of years before even the earliest agglutination of Judaism. The skulls of antiquity which have been exhumed afford proofs of this, which, like the records of the rocks, can no longer admit of the slightest doubt. For example, many of the old Egyptian, Greek, and Roman crania, indicate a very high order of moral development, and if those nations had had the benefits of modern science, they would doubtless have evolved a civilization which would put to the blush any that has been known since the advent of Christianity. And even as it was, with their limited advantages, look at the magnificent culture of pagan Greece and Rome. True, they had their vices, but so have we to-day; and if the absence of flagrant vices and crimes should be necessary to entitle a nation to be called civilized, what would future historians say of us? However, the immorality of the ancient pagans, as compared with their virtues, has been greatly exaggerated, and the fact can not be disputed away that every moral principle asserted by the Church to have been original with Christ, was not only proclaimed centuries before he was born, but by people who lived independently of, and even prior to, the Jews. This matter is set at rest by facts of established history as well as by the most recent archæological researches.

In opposing Christianity, therefore, as a religious system, we denounce simply its pernicious doctrines and absurd dogmas which are contradicted by science and plainly inimical to the highest happiness of mankind. Among these are chiefly the existence of a personal God and a personal Devil, the fall of man, the scheme of salvation by faith, and endless torment to those who reject Christ as a divine savior. It is these superstitions, together with the institutions founded upon them, which constitute Christianity a distinct system of religion, and, I repeat, it is these alone which Infidelity discredits and desires to supersede.

As a substitute for the hypothesis of a personal creator, we submit the proposition that the universe in its entirety is eternal and self-existent. Instead of ascribing the wonderful phenomena of nature to a cause even more inexplicable than the phenomena themselves, we regard the universe as the self-contained cause of its activities, in the same general sense that theologians imagine God as the self-contained cause of his operations. We hold that this is the only reasonable view, from the fact that every form of argument indicating the necessity of an antecedent or creative cause of nature, would also imply the necessity of an antecedent cause of that creator. We are, therefore, logically driven to the conclusion that matter contains within itself the potency to produce all the effects which we be hold.

It is idle for Christians to complain that Materialism degrades man to the level of bricks and mortar. Properly defined, our principles not only detract nothing from man, but, on the contrary, give him a greater dignity than he has ever enjoyed hitherto. On this point, Mr. Underwood well says:

"No wonder theologians bestow upon matter so many bad names when they have divested it of its noblest powers and capacities in order to enhance the greatness of a being who is supposed to act through it. In their estimation, it is inert, powerless, contemptible, unless stirred like the pool of Bethesda by the potent touch of Jehovah. Let them restore to it the powers of which it has been robbed in order to enrich a being whose glory has ever been at the cost of the world and humanity, and possibly they will see less reason for maligning it. They may then be able to see in it those elements which in their ever-varying forms become not only the air they breathe, the water they drink, and the food which hunger craves; not only the amethyst and diamond, the violet, lily, and rosebud, but the ruby lip, the love-lit eye, the wonderful brain, and, in brief, the bodies and souls of the noblest beings that the earth has yet produced."

Our doctrine is simply this: Every force is a quality, condition, or activity of matter, hence neither is conceivable apart from some form of the other. All who admit this to be true are Materialists in every proper sense of the term. Theology, on the other hand, teaches the existence of forces as entities wholly independent of matter, and the original creation of matter from nothing; ideas which are not only incomprehensible, but directly opposed to every principle of reason. Thus, we recognize no such thing as absolutely dead matter. Every atom is endowed from eternity with some force, some phase or degree of intelligence, and the more refined, complex, and subtile the combination of matter, the higher will be the manifestation of life and mentality. If any thing whatever could be eternally self-existent, surely living matter could be. We have thus no need of a creator.

However, no one will admit more freely than the Infidel, that the fear of God often has the effect of a moral restraint, or that through a loving desire to please this imaginary being, many are encouraged to lead noble lives. But merely because this belief sometimes produces salutary effects, it does not necessarily follow that it is natural or healthful. The man who does right simply from fear of incurring the ill-will of the Deity, is at heart essentially dishonest, and, in the scale of moral development, no higher than a savage. The only truly noble aim in right conduct is to increase the happiness of mankind; and he who does right from this motive thereby directly strengthens his Benevolence, and tends to bring all his lower propensities under the control of his moral sentiments. Whereas, virtuous actions flowing simply from a desire to secure the favor of a being whom it would be impossible to harm, could only intensify our selfish faculties, or, at the best, excite a blind and purposeless sense of justice. It is thus obvious that the incentives furnished by Humanitarianism to goodness and purity, are higher than those of theology.

However, it will probably be objected that we have nothing to take the place of Christ as an ideal or model for our imitation. To this we would say that Phrenology reveals every principle regarding the supremacy of moral sentiment and intellect that is to be found exemplified in the character of Christ, with this advantage, that the teachings of Phrenology are much higher, inasmuch as they condemn and refute the infamous system of revenge involved in Christ's doctrine of eternal retribution, and inculcate a principle of government which does not outrage the moral sense. It is true the excuse is often made by liberal Christians that the doctrine of Hell is not warranted by a correct interpretation of the Scriptures, and some assert that the passages supporting it can be shown to have been interpolated. If this can be established at all, it will only establish too much for the life of orthodoxy. For if the Bible was written by divine inspiration, and God permitted those interpolations to paralyze mankind with fear, and for eighteen centuries to redden the earth with blood, how can it be said that he is less responsible for the misunderstanding of his will than if he had written the interpolated words with his own hand? The orthodox masses still cherish this souvenir of our quadrupedal ancestry, and, for the most part, undoubtedly believe it. This is a sufficient reason for our opposing it.

Those who would be interested in a further explanation of the phrenological theory of moral government, will find much of value pertaining to the subject in George Combe's "Constitution of Man," the best book, in my opinion, ever written by a theist. If the words Deity and Creative Wisdom, employed by Mr. Combe, were replaced by the terms Nature and Evolution, this remarkable work would be almost a complete exposition of the highest Materialistic philosophy. Mr. Combe was a Unitarian, and an Infidel to the orthodoxy of his time, and while we do not indorse his theism to-day, we must acknowledge our great indebtedness to him for his splendid contributions to the cause of humanity. For myself, I gladly take this opportunity to say that I regard him as one of the noblest men the world has yet produced.

To secure an object of worship, there is no need to anthropomorphize the absolute, and bow down to the unknown. And since the qualities Christians admire in their conceptions of Deity are simply the best elements of human nature, we hold that the chief object of our reverence and respect, should be the ideal man, *as revealed to us by mental science*, while humanity should receive all our labor and affection. In order to love a conceptional God, the individual must first possess a moral nature; but how much more deeply and intensely his sympathies will respond when, instead of catering to the imaginary caprices of an infinite Omnipotence, he turns to the suffering millions of his fellow men. It is often asserted that we may love both God and humanity. True; but no theist can fully appreciate his duty to those around him until he realizes the dependence of man upon himself.

God is but a shadow. Man is the substance. For the imaginary we would substitute the real. For the invisible we would give the visible. In the place of theology, anthropology.

Rejecting the notion that a Devil, or fallen angel, is the originator of the disorder and misery in this world, we hold that what is called evil is simply the result of non-adjustment to our environments. There is no such thing as evil in the abstract. It is always relative, and quite frequently the very circumstances and conditions which operate adversely to one person result in great good to another.

In place of the belief that sin first entered the human "heart" through Satan, and that malignant spirits now influence men to do wrong, we submit the entire facts of phrenological science, which prove that the depravity in human nature is due entirely to conditions of cerebral development and susceptibility. In a word, that organization determines character.

Instead of the doctrine that man is now in a "fallen state," and incapable of attaining the highest moral development without the aid of supernatural forces, we are prepared to show by indisputable facts of history, as well as by the demonstrations of science, that the human race has risen, not fallen, and that instead of supernatural aids to development, all that is necessary is obedience to the laws or methods of nature. To this end, we would encourage a popular study of anthropology in general, but especially Phrenology. We would have young persons made as familiar with the laws of marriage adaptation, hereditary transmission, sexual physiology, mental development, hygiene, etc., etc., as they now are with the details of their supernatural creeds.

It is a vain excuse to say that only a small proportion of the people would ever be interested in these subjects. The difficulty now is that the minds of the people are too greatly warped and misled by the chimerical doctrines of the Bible to be able to appreciate anthropology. But let the masses be once entirely freed from theological views of life, and taught the true sources of happiness, and we shall see a revolution in sociology. When the people once discover what advantages are to be gained by a knowledge of these things, they can not fail to be interested in them.  If governed by selfish motives alone, they could not do otherwise.  And then, when the conditions of bodily and mental health are understood, it will be but a short step to the observance of them.  The day will come when men and women will be ashamed to be the parents of such mental and physical dwarfs as the majority of children are to-day.  Public opinion will be brought to bear on the subject of senseless marriages, and it will have greater effect than any of the ghostly terrors of theology.  We shall then have fewer children and fuller orbed, for they will be the offspring of a purer love, and will be governed by reason and kindness, instead of a whip in this world and threats of endless torment after death.

And here allow me to remark that Materialism gives no encouragement to vice, and no sanction to laxity in punishing criminals.  In suggesting reform in the present system of criminal legislation and management of children, we refer only to the question of method.  Capital punishment, the doctrine of Hell, and violence to children, all belong together. They were all born of that part of the brain which man has in common with hyenas and snakes. To adopt an illustration from Combe, if one dog steals a bone from another, Combativeness and Destructiveness are immediately excited in the owner of the bone, and (provided he has the requisite physical endowments,) he proceeds to inflict a severe chastisement upon the thief, after which, he sets him loose without any inquiry into the causes which led to the offense, and without any thought as to the ultimate consequences to the offender. Men act on the same principle. If a burglary or murder is committed and the culprit arrested, a trial is immediately instituted with the sole view of ascertaining his guilt. And if the evidence is found sufficient, the offender is simply ordered to be flogged, fined, imprisoned, banished, or hanged, as the case may be, and, except in the event of the death penalty, after the infliction of the punishment, the culprit is turned adrift upon society, perhaps soon to repeat his crime with more malice in his heart and with less respect for the law than he ever felt before.

What we would substitute for this animal retaliation, is a kind of imprisonment and compulsory subjection to useful labor and elevating influences, which should be modified according to the causes of the crime and with a purpose of improving the criminal. Only those who are unacquainted with the principles of mental science will object that such a method would not be as efficient as the one commonly practiced now. To be sure, the reform we are advocating relates especially to capital punishment and the whipping of children. Whatever penalties are inflicted, however, should undoubtedly be executed with great thoroughness and care. But we may be certain that the animal method arouses only the basest instincts of the mind, while the moral system appeals to the highest faculties.

Perhaps the most plausible objection to our theory of punishment is, that many individuals are too brutal to be susceptible to any moral influence. This we admit; but can the Bible do any more for such cases than we? Does the Church convert or restrain idiots or madmen? For all incorrigible subjects we suggest permanent confinement, and there can be no excuse for willful violence to such unfortunate beings. Conversation with criminals will reveal the fact that to the average wrongdoer the prospect of imprisonment for life is quite as much of a restraint as the gallows, and the real secret of the popular desire for capital punishment is a thirst for revenge, which is fostered and encouraged by the spirit of orthodoxy.

However, I do not wish to appear dogmatic in these remarks, and I freely admit that very many persons uphold capital punishment from a sincere conviction that it is necessary for the protection of society. But whether it is necessary or not in our present stage of development, there can surely be no harm in discussing the subject from a philosophical point of view, and acquainting ourselves with a principle which it will be our duty to observe whenever and wherever our civilization shall render it practicable.

I can also anticipate a denial from many readers, that the "spirit of orthodoxy" promotes cruelty and violence. In debating the subject of Christianity its advocates are accustomed to define it as the doctrine of a pure life; the principle of universal love and forgiveness, etc. But when they teach it from the pulpit or in their ecclesiastical tribunals, it becomes transformed into a system of dogmas, many of which have not only no connection with any principle of morality, but are simply infamous and deadly. When Christians expound their religion let them spurn every disguise and appear under their dual flag. We do not deny that there is a noble and lofty side to Christianity, but when pure water flows into a polluted stream, the whole becomes defiled. Thus, while the Bible teaches forgiveness, the doctrine that unbelievers are deserving of eternal pain is adapted only to distort and undermine every idea of true justice. How can a man have any clear conception of equity who is educated to sympathize with such a dogma? Indeed, how can Christians be expected to improve on the example set them by their Master? Can they forgive and love their enemies when they believe that Christ is going to damn his forever? Belief in such notions regarding man's responsibility to a supposed Creator, is sure to foster sympathy with them. And what men love they will be likely to practice, so that those who favor an infamous punishment in another and endless existence, will be almost certain to have perverted and unjust views regarding methods of government in the affairs of this world.

Thus, instead of salvation from Hell in an imaginary hereafter, by faith in the dogmas of the Church, we offer salvation from the evils in this world by patient and industrious attention to the conditions of development, health, and happiness, as revealed by science. Instead of vainly trying to restrain men from vice and crime by the fear of punishment after death, we would teach them the certainty with which they will be punished in this world for every essentially immoral act they commit. We would teach them that whether their sins are found out or not, they can not do wrong without robbing themselves and stepping backward toward the old four-footed life. And if we fail to produce any evidence of a heaven of perpetual joy, we can at least offer the happy assurance that not one poor human soul will ever suffer an eternity of pain.

Properly defined, religion means simply the bond between man and the highest object which he can love, and toward which he can feel a sense of duty sufficiently strong to discipline all his faculties, and prescribe to him a rule of life. Hence, it is right that in this sense we should have a religion. But instead of the God of the Bible as the chief object of our consideration, we would devote our efforts to our fellow men, and make the sense of our obligation to them, if not to ourselves, curb every tendency to evil. Those who could be insensible to such a religion as this, would be callous to every thing good in the religion of Christ. There can be no really lofty motive in worshiping a conditionless, infinite being of whom we can form no clear conception, or at least whom we could neither benefit nor injure. But we can add to the happiness of mankind, and in so doing we exercise all our highest and noblest powers. This, then, is our substitute. Instead of God, we would live and labor for mankind. Instead of Christianity, the Religion of Humanity.

FINIS.

www.ingramcontent.com/pod-product-compliance
Lightning Source LLC
Chambersburg PA
CBHW032100220426
**43664CB00008B/1074**